explore...

Point Lobos State Reserve

by Jeff Thomson

Dear Margaret and Jeff –
Thanks for your help and support
Good friends like you are hard
to find!

Jeff

DISCLAIMER

The author has made every effort to assure that the information in this book is accurate as of date of publication. However, park features can change over time. Expect that some changes have occurred.

The author and publisher assumes no liability from damage or loss arising from errors or omissions, if any, in this book and is not responsible for personal injury, damage to property or violation of law in connection with the use of this book.

The reader assumes personal responsibility for his/her safety while visiting the reserve. Be cautious and exercise common sense.

Published by
Walkabout Publications
P.O. Box 1299
Soquel, CA 95073
(408) 462-3370

Text Copyright © 1997 by Jeff Thomson
FIRST EDITION 1997
Printed in the United States
of America on recycled paper

Design – Bert J. Ihlenfeld
Inside cover photo –
   China Cove: Jeff Thomson
Back cover photos –
   Cypress Cove: Jeff Thomson
   Purple sea urchin: Jerry Loomis
   Sea otter: Richard Bucich
Map – Copyright © Patrick Santana
Illustrations – Copyright © Fran Ciesla
Illustrations remain property
of the original copyright holder

All photos are used by permission.

ISBN Number 0-9636945-3-7
Library of Congress Catalog Card
Number 97-60476

Acknowledgements

I want to thank the many kind and generous people whose contributions made this book possible.

First of all, I want to thank my wife Debbie for her constant encouragement and unfailing moral support. My appreciation for her help goes far beyond what words can express. Supervising Ranger Glen McGowen and his staff were especially generous with their time and always available to answer questions and provide resource information. I owe a special debt of gratitude to Bonni Weinstein and Carol Maehr who spent countless hours reviewing the manuscript. Their understanding and appreciation of the reserve is truly extraordinary. I also want to thank Kurt Loesch for reviewing the text for historical accuracy. Special thanks go to Mary Riley-Whisler, Marilyn Kodani, Ted Ciesla, Kit Salisbury and Jeff and Margaret Hicks.

I am extremely grateful for the help of these fine people.

Table of Contents

introduction

Superlatives abound when it comes to describing Point Lobos State Reserve: spectacular, dramatic and inspiring are but a few that come quickly to mind. Volumes have been written about this rare and exceptional place, yet perhaps the most appropriate words are contained in a simple statement by landscape artist Francis McComas "...the greatest meeting of land and water in the world."

Located on California's central coast, just a few miles south of Carmel and Monterey, Point Lobos is truly a place of unsurpassed natural beauty. Wind-sculpted Monterey cypress trees cling to sheer granite headlands high above the pounding surf. An ever-changing pattern of wave-carved coves reveal picturesque white sand beaches with emerald-green waters. Tide pools along the surf-washed shore lure the visitor to explore fascinating life in the intertidal zone. Miles of hiking trails trace the ocean shore, probe the oak and pine forests or wind along open meadows resplendent with seasonal wildflowers.

The visual beauty of Point Lobos is just one aspect of what makes this place so special. The reserve is also home to an amazing number of both land and ocean animals, some that live here all year and others which visit on annual migrations. Whale watching is a popular activity between December and May, when Pacific gray whales travel close to Point Lobos as they journey south to breed in the warm water of lagoons on the west coast of Baja California, Mexico, then retrace their path north to summer feeding grounds off the coast of Alaska. The reserve is also home for a year-round population of southern sea otters, harbor seals and California sea lions. In fact, it was the almost incessant barking of the sea lions which led early Spanish explorers to name the point Punta de Los Lobos Marinos, Point of the Sea Wolves.

The value of preserving the natural and scenic qualities of this extraordinary place led the State of California to acquire Point Lobos in 1933. Then, in 1960, 750 underwater acres surrounding Point Lobos were added to create the nation's first marine reserve. Beyond the borders of the state marine reserve is the Monterey Bay National Marine Sanctuary, the largest marine sanctuary in the nation. It stretches 300 miles along the California coast and includes one of North America's largest underwater canyons.

Often called the "crown jewel" of the California State Park system, Point Lobos has been visited by millions of people. Each and every one of them has taken home a special memory of this oasis in a hurried world. Come and experience for yourself the treasures of this rare and exceptional place.

The view from North Point.   Photo: Jeff Thomson

for your information

Point Lobos is one of a number of California State Reserves created to embrace natural or scenic characteristics of statewide significance. The purpose of a state reserve is to preserve native ecological associations, unique animal and plant life, geological features and scenic qualities in an undisturbed condition.

Getting to the Reserve

The reserve is located on California Highway 1, about six miles south of Monterey and approximately three miles south of Carmel. During the summer months, public transportation is available. Call Monterey-Salinas Transit at 408-424-7695 for bus schedule information.

Weather

The climate at Point Lobos is best described as maritime Mediterranean with typically cool summers and relatively warm winters. In the summer, coastal fog is common between June and August, while winter rains generally occur from mid-November to April, with January and February being the wettest months.

Picnic Areas

The reserve has three picnic areas furnished with tables, water fountains and restroom facilities. All are located in scenic areas near the ocean and are accessible by automobile.

Whalers Cove Picnic Area: This site is nestled against the granite cliffs at historic Whalers Cove, where you will also find interpretive panels with photos and descriptions of some of the plants and animals living in the underwater reserve. The Whalers Cabin and Whaling Station Museums are located nearby.

Piney Woods Picnic Area: This picnic area is the largest at the reserve and is located a short distance inland from the coastline.

Bird Island Picnic Area: Located near the southern end of the reserve, short trails lead from this site to picturesque China Cove and the white sands of Gibson Beach.

The Information Station

Visitors will find an Information Station located at the Sea Lion Point Parking Area. It has interpretive panels, literature about the reserve and volunteer docents available to answer questions. The docents also lead informative tours which present introductions to the history, geology and natural history of the reserve.

Interpretive Museums

Whalers Cabin: Constructed in the early 1850s by Chinese fishermen, the Whalers Cabin is staffed by docents and houses several interesting exhibits that document the rich cultural history of Point Lobos.

Whaling Station: Between 1862 and 1879, Whalers Cove was the site of a shore whaling station operated by a company of Portuguese sea-

men. This new museum, located next to the Whalers Cabin, contains displays of whaling equipment and exhibit panels describing the lives of the whalers and their families.

Whalers cabin.   Photo: Jeff Thomson

Scuba Diving

Access to the 750-acre underwater reserve is located at Whalers Cove. Facilities include vehicle parking, restrooms, a cement ramp and water hose. All divers and boats must register at the ranger station. For more information see the reserve regulations chapter of this book.

Access For People With Disabilities

While most of the trails are classified as easy, none of them are fully accessible. However, trail improvements to make portions of the Sea Lion Point and Sand Hill trails wheelchair accessible are underway. Restroom facilities that are accessible include those at Whalers Cove, Sea Lion Point Parking Area (portable facility) and Piney Woods Picnic Area.

reserve regulations

The following regulations are intended to enhance your enjoyment of the reserve and to protect its natural beauty.

Hours: The reserve is open all year from 9:00 am to 5:00 pm. During summer, the closing time is extended to 7:00 pm.

Entry: An entrance fee is charged for all vehicles. There is no charge for those entering on foot.

To enhance the quality of your visit and to protect the reserve's resources, visitor numbers are limited to 450 people at any one time. On busy days, visitors may wait in line to enter on a one-vehicle-out, one-vehicle-in basis.

Motor Vehicles: The speed limit in the reserve is 15 miles per hour. There are nine parking areas, so if one is full, please drive to another. Always park head in. Vehicles over 20 feet in length may enter only when traffic is light and may be turned away on weekends, school vacations or holidays, and during the summer months. Trailers or motorhomes towing vehicles are not allowed. Busses are allowed on a limited basis.

Dogs: Are not allowed in the reserve with the exception of service dogs for the blind or physically impaired.

Wildlife: All of the animals within the reserve are wild and should not be disturbed. Do not feed any animals including squirrels (they bite) and birds. Also, stay back at least 50 feet from any marine mammals that have "hauled out" on the beaches or rocky outcroppings. Please be aware that it is against federal law to disturb any marine mammals and significant fines are imposed for violations.

Fishing: Is prohibited within the boundary of the marine reserve.

Scuba Diving: Is allowed at Whalers Cove and Bluefish Cove. Diving access is limited to Whalers Cove. All scuba divers and snorklers

Photo: Jerry Loomis

must register at the ranger station and obtain a permit. There is a fee per dive team. Diving permits are limited to 15 teams on any given day. Each permit is limited to not more than three nor less than two divers and is valid only for the date issued. Reservations can be made as much as two months in advance or as little as one day in advance. To make scuba diving reservations, call the reserve's E-mail address: PtLobos@mbay.net or telephone the voicemail/fax at (408) 624-8413.

Collecting: Do not collect, disturb or remove any natural object. This includes all natural features such as rocks, shells, flowers, tidepool life, etc.

Smoking: Smoking is allowed only in the picnic areas, parking lots and on paved roads.

Fires: Fires of any kind are not allowed and stove use is prohibited.

Picnicking: Is allowed only in the established picnic areas.

Games: Activities like frisbee, kite flying, softball, etc. are not compatible with the purpose of a state reserve and are not allowed at Point Lobos. These activities are welcomed at Carmel River State Beach north of the reserve.

Trails: Remain on established trails and within wire guides. Permitted exceptions are the shorelines at Moss Cove and Sea Lion Point, the shoreline between Sand Hill Cove and Weston Beach, Gibson Beach, China Cove and Hidden Beach.

Bicycle Use: Bicycles are allowed only on paved roads. There are posts in the major parking areas where visitors can lock their bikes. Walking your bicycle on the trails is prohibited.

For Your Safety

Poison Oak: Is abundant in the reserve and so are ticks. Stay on the trails to avoid both.

Respect the Sea: Be aware of large unexpected waves that can knock you down and sweep you out to sea. When you are near the shoreline, the cardinal rule is never turn your back to the ocean.

Lock your car and keep your valuables with you.

history

While Point Lobos is justifiably famous for its scenic beauty and remarkable diversity of plants and wildlife, it is also a place rich in human history. Over the past 150 years, this area has played host to a virtual parade of human activity. At one time or another, Point Lobos has been home to Chinese fishermen, Japanese abalone harvesters and Portuguese whalers. It has also been the site of an abalone cannery, coal mining business, granite quarry, military base and numerous film productions.

The First Inhabitants

Several thousand years before the first European explorers arrived in 1602, the coastal area of central California was inhabited by triblets of indigenous people known collectively as the Ohlone. Each triblet, averaging about 200 people, had one or more permanent villages usually consisting of dome-shaped thatched huts clustered around an open area. Here at Point Lobos, the Ohlone established spring and summer village sites near the mouth of San Jose Creek at the reserve's northern boundary and along Gibson Creek, which forms the southern edge of the reserve. Their village along San Jose Creek, known as Ichxenta, was first occupied about 2,500 to 3,000 years ago, and is thought to be the longest inhabited Ohlone village site in the Monterey area.

The Ohlone enjoyed a plentiful food supply of acorns, birds and mammals from the nearby mountains, as well as fish from the ocean and local streams. Within the reserve, 19 sites have been identified which were used as seasonal camps while gathering abalone and mussels or grinding seeds and acorns into meal. Today, signs of the Ohlone's former presence can be found in many forms: black dirt from years of campsite fires, grinding stones, and large mounds of cast-away shells, called middens.

The Spanish and Mexican Periods

The Ohlone living near Point Lobos may have been the first indigenous people encountered by Spanish exploring expeditions, beginning in 1602 when Sebastian Vizcaino's ship entered Carmel Bay. About 170 years later, the Portola expedition on the move north from

San Diego camped along San Jose Creek. Portola's assignment was to find a route from Mexico (then part of the Spanish empire) to Monterey and, along the way, locate suitable places to establish the soon-to-follow missions and military camps called presidios. This expedition also ushered in the Spanish Colonial period of California history which lasted until 1822.

The second of 21 Spanish missions was established at Monterey in 1770, but within a year it was moved to Carmel and named San Carlos Borromeo de Carmelo. The mission's cowboys, or vaqueros, tended herds of cattle on the nearby grasslands and became the first nonnative people to use what is now Point Lobos State Reserve property. It was also during the era of Spanish occupation that Point Lobos was first named, when the barking of sea lions inspired the name Punta de los Lobos Marinos, Point of the Sea Wolves.

Soon after Mexico gained its independence from Spain in 1822, the new government began a policy of awarding land grants to loyal Mexican citizens, one of whom was Don Marcelino Escobar, a distinguished official in Monterey. The property that now makes up the reserve was once part of an 8,818 acre grant given to Escobar in 1839. A couple of years later, the land was sold to Dona Josefa de Abrego for $250, or about 3 cents an acre. Dona Josefa held onto the property for about a year. Then, in a curious transaction where no money changed hands, she deeded the land to a group of soldiers stationed at the Monterey Presidio. The soldiers maintained possession of the land for six months, then in 1844 gave it to their superior officer, Jose Castro. After California was annexed from Mexico by the United States in 1848, Castro's claim to the land was reviewed by a commission established to sort out the multiple claims to private property in the new territory. Complicating matters further, Castro sold the land, other claims to the property were filed, and it was not until 1888 that this tangled web was settled by a patent signed by President Grover Cleveland. After everything was said and done, the original Mexican land grant had been divided into 34 parcels. A month after President Cleveland signed the patent, several owners of the parcels in and around Point Lobos sold their interests to the Carmelo Land and Coal Company. Now, for the first time in 45 years, most of the old rancho including Point Lobos was under single ownership.

Historic sketch of "try works" at Whalers Cove c. 1863.

Whaling Activities at Point Lobos

Portuguese whalers from the Azore Islands arrived at Point Lobos in 1862 and set up living quarters on the east side of Whalers Cove. Comprising one of 16 shore whaling stations established on the west coast of California, the whalers and their families made up a small community of 50-60 people. About 15-20 men were part of a crew that hunted gray whales which migrate along the California coast between mid-December and May. From the top of Whalers Knoll, a lookout would spot passing whales, then raise a flag to signal the crews down at the cove. Open-top boats were rowed out to sea where the men would try their luck with harpoons. If a whale was killed, it was towed back to the cove, hoisted out of the water and its blubber sliced into large strips. Next the blubber was cut into smaller chunks and melted in large iron cauldrons called "try pots", to produce an oil used primarily for lamp fuel. With the advent of kerosene lamps in the late 1880s, demand for whale oil slacked off and the local whaling industry fell on hard times. There was a brief revival of whaling operations at Point Lobos in 1897 when a Japanese company set up business, but this operation lasted only a few years.

The Whaling Station Museum at Whalers Cove documents the historic whaling activities at Point Lobos with displays of whaling equipment and exhibit panels describing the lives of the whalers and their families. Next to the museum, you can see two of the old try pots used to boil whale blubber and view part of an almost 100-year-old fin-back whale skeleton.

Abalone Harvesting

As you walk along the reserve's trails, chances are good that you will find fragments of iridescent abalone shell scattered about. The rocky shores of Point Lobos provide a perfect habitat for this muscular mollusk. Abalone meat has long been considered a delicacy in many cultures and its shell prized for use as mother-of-pearl furniture inlay and the manufacture of jewelry and buttons. While the Ohlone gathered abalone at Point Lobos, it was not until the Chinese arrived in the early 1850s that it was harvested commercially.

Soon after the California gold rush of 1849, historians believe a small group of Chinese fishermen and their families set sail from southern China in 30-foot junks. Following the prevailing winds and ocean currents, they probably arrived at Point Lobos around 1851 and established what may be the first Chinese fishing settlement in California. By 1853 more Chinese arrived from the gold fields and settled along the coast at nearby Monterey. Word quickly spread about the abundant abalone beds and before long several hundred Chinese were engaged in the local abalone harvesting business. They also under-

stood the rich potential of the sea and diversified their catch to include squid, sea urchins and a variety of fish. The Chinese settlement at Point Lobos consisted of about a dozen buildings, one of which remains and now houses the Whalers Cabin Museum.

In the mid-1890s, a young marine biologist from Japan, Gennosuke Kodani, arrived at Point Lobos to investigate reports of rich beds of abalone in the area and soon sent for workers from his native village of Chiba. At first, abalone near the shore were harvested and dried in

Abalone diver c. 1915.
Photo: Pat Hathaway Photo Collection

the sun on wooden racks set up along Coal Chute Point at the north side of Whalers Cove. As the supply of shallow-water abalone dwindled, the workers donned hard-hat diving suits and ventured out on boats into deeper water. Using hand-powered pumps to supply air to the divers, the Japanese at Point Lobos pioneered an industry that eventually spread up and down the California coast.

Abalone cannery c. 1920.   Photo: Pat Hathaway Photo Collection

Around 1899, Kodani formed a partnership with Alexander Allan, who had recently purchased the property that now forms the reserve, and together they established an abalone cannery which was located at what is now the Whalers Cove Parking Area. The cannery was so successful it eventually accounted for 75% of the abalone sold in California. It stayed in operation until 1928, and was dismantled in 1933 when the property became a state reserve. The Kodani family home was located near Coal Chute Point and is shown on the reserve's map as Kodani Village.

Although abalone meat was popular in eastern cultures, it was not considered a gourmet item by most Americans until the 1920s, when a new recipe developed by "Pop" Doelter, a local restaurant owner, caught on and the abalone "steak" was introduced to the American palate. Doelter used the Whalers Cabin as his processing plant from 1918 to 1920.

Coal chute bunker and tramway. Note the abalone drying on racks in the foreground c. 1904.   Photo: Pat Hathaway Photo Collection

Coal Mining

In the mid-1870s, coal was discovered in the coastal hills just a few miles southeast of Point Lobos. After being mined, the coal was hauled by horse-drawn wagons to the old county road, east of what is now Highway 1. It was then loaded into ore carts which traveled along a short tramway to a coal chute built on a rocky point at the north side of Whalers Cove. The deep water of what is now called Coal Chute Point allowed coastal steamships close access to the point where they took on their load. The Carmel Land and Coal Company operated until the late 1890s when poor market conditions combined with high operating costs forced the mine to close. Behind the Whalers Cabin Museum, you will find an old ore cart similar to those used in that operation.

The Quarries

In 1855, a granite quarry was established at what is now the Whalers Cove Parking Area. Point Lobos granite was used to build the U.S. Mint in San Francisco and the Navy shipyards at Mare Island in San Francisco Bay.

About 30 years later, a gravel quarry was operating at the Pit, a small cove nestled between Coal Chute Point and Granite Point. Today, visitors can walk on the Pit's gravel beach and trace the old haul road, now the Moss Cove Trail, to the reserve's northern boundary at Monastery Beach.

The War Years

It may be hard to imagine, but Point Lobos was once the site of "secret" military operations. By the summer of 1942 both the U.S. Army and Air Force occupied the reserve, which was closed to civilians for the duration of World War II.

As early as December of 1941, a unit of the U.S. Army Coastal Defense Squad set up anti-aircraft gun emplacements and used the Whalers Cabin as their headquarters. They were followed in August of 1942 by the 4th Air Force Signal Corps Unit which used the reserve as a site for their long-range radar equipment. Eighty men from this unit were housed in a tent camp located near the reserve's entrance station and a radar station was installed on Whalers Knoll. While crude by today's standards, the radar station used the best technology available at that time and could detect objects as far as 150 miles away.

In 1943, the Army used Whalers Cove as the site of a school to train soldiers of the 543rd Amphibious Brigade in the use of amphibious landing craft. Their drills included landing the boats on the beach, then scrambling up to the meadow. This brigade was subsequently involved in 60 landings in the Southwest Pacific.

Evangeline movie set on fire c. 1929.
Photo: Pat Hathaway Photo Collection

Lights – Camera – Action!

Between 1914 and 1989, 45 movies were filmed "on location" at or near Point Lobos State Reserve. Some of the most famous actors and actresses in American film history were part of these productions, including Erich von Stronheim, Mary Pickford, Douglas Fairbanks, Greer Garson, James Cagney, Richard Burton and Dustin Hoffman, to name just a few.

Unfortunately, some of the glamour associated with Hollywood coming to Point Lobos came with a price to the environment. In 1929, a movie set for the film Evangeline was constructed at Headland Cove, then was burned down as part of the film's plot. The resulting fire burned trees, brush and grassland in the surrounding area to the extent that the scars from this fire are still evident today.

A Park is Born

Beginning in 1890, a series of events began to unfold which would eventually lead to the establishment of today's state reserve. Coal mining near Point Lobos had become unprofitable, so the Carmel Land and Coal Company subdivided the area around Whalers Cove into 1,000 residential lots

Satie and Alexander Allan
Courtesy: Mary Whisler

for a development that was first named Point Lobos City but which soon became known as Carmelito.

Several years after the Carmelito subdivision was laid out, an engineer from Illinois, Alexander M. Allan, purchased 640 acres of the mining company's property at Point Lobos. Already a successful race track architect and real estate developer, Allan moved into a ranch house at Point Lobos in 1898 and set about to repurchase the Carmelito lots which had already been sold. Allan, like many others, recognized that Point Lobos was a unique and special place which should be preserved. Concerned over the environmental impact of an ever-increasing number of visitors interested in seeing the cypress trees and scenic coastline, Allan and his wife, Satie, set up a toll gate, prohibited camping, and allowed picnic fires only in specified areas.

Meanwhile, interest in preserving Point Lobos as a national or state park was gaining momentum. As scientists and foresters studied the Monterey cypress trees growing at Point Lobos and Cypress Point on the north side of Carmel Bay, they realized these trees do not naturally grow anywhere else in the world. By the mid-1920s, the Save-the-Redwoods League was actively involved in an effort to preserve the Monterey cypress. They hired the internationally known landscape architect, Frederick Law Olmstead, to research Point Lobos and report on the areas most worthy of preservation. Olmstead's report described Point Lobos as "the most outstanding example on the coast of California of picturesque rock and surf scenery in combination with unique vegetation, including typical Monterey cypress." With assistance from the Save-the-Redwoods League, the State of California purchased 348 acres at Point Lobos from the Allan family in 1933. Another 15 acres of cypress-covered headlands were given to the state by the Allan family and dedicated as a memorial to Alexander and Satie Allan. Further land additions have expanded the reserve to almost 400 acres now open to the public. In 1960, 750 underwater acres were added to create the first marine reserve in the United States. The marine reserve was designated an ecological reserve in 1973, and in 1992 became part of the Monterey Bay National Marine Sanctuary, the nation's largest marine sanctuary.

geology

The "modern" geological history of Point Lobos begins about 100 million years ago when dinosaurs still roamed the earth. Miles below the earth's surface, a molten mass of rock deep inside a prehistoric chain of active volcanoes slowly cooled into what geologists call Santa Lucia Granodiorite. Over the next 40 million years this hard, granite-like rock rose to the surface and now comprises one of the four types of rock at Point Lobos. Resting on the granodiorite is an ancient deposit of sand and gravel that formed about 60 million years ago and has since hardened into a sandstone called the Carmelo Formation. Lying on top of the Carmelo Formation, like frosting on a cake, is the third geologically significant type of rock found at the reserve: sedimentary rocks that were deposited on ancient marine terraces. These terraces formed as ocean waves created wide platforms when the sea level was higher than it is today. The sediments that eroded from the old shoreline and deposited on the marine terraces consist of clay, silt, sand and gravel up to two million years old. The fourth type of rock at Point Lobos is found along the shoreline where you can see how wave action has worn away the Carmelo Formation and granodiorite to form deposits of gravel and white sand beaches.

To best understand and appreciate the geology of Point Lobos, it is useful to have a basic understanding of plate tectonics. According to this commonly-accepted geological theory, the earth's crust is divided into several large rigid blocks or plates that float like giant rafts on a core of semi-molten rock. As the earth sheds its heat, these plates move and shift position, accounting for the occurrence of continental drift, earthquakes and volcanoes. As recently as 70 million years ago (a mere blip on the geologic time scale) the Santa Lucia Granodiorite here at the reserve was once located approximately 1,200 miles to the south, near the tip of Baja California, Mexico. Tectonic forces then ripped away a huge block of the earth's crust containing the granodiorite, and over the next 20 million years transported it northward an extraordinary distance of almost 1,000 miles. While this large piece of rock that geologists have named the Salinian block was moving north, it was also pushed upward, temporarily exposing the granodiorite above the water and allowing rivers and streams to erode a system of valleys and canyons.

Carmelo formation. Photo: Jeff Thomson

Around 60 million years ago, the Salinian block subsided and ocean waters filled the granodiorite canyons. On land, ancient rivers carried lava from distant volcanoes down to the shoreline, and along the way scoured it into rounded pebbles and cobblestone-sized rocks. Over time, these rocks and layers of sand were deposited on the submarine canyon walls by underwater landslides and eventually cemented into a conglomerate called the Carmelo Formation. For many people, the Carmelo Formation is the most interesting type of rock at Point Lobos. It is softer than the granodiorite and is easily seen along the south shore of the reserve, where it has been eroded by ocean waves to form a photogenic series of coves, crevices and shelves.

The next significant period of Point Lobos geological history begins about 20 million years ago when tectonic forces once again moved this plate of the earth's crust upward and another 250 miles north to its present location. Then, with the coming of the ice ages which began around two million years ago, these rocks were exposed to the sun and eroded by rain, then submerged again as the sea level waxed and waned.

When the sea stayed at one level for a long period, marine terraces and sloping cliffs along the shoreline were formed, and are still evident today. The most noticeable marine terraces at Point Lobos formed between 35 and 10 thousand years ago. The older terrace developed its shoreline at an elevation of about 125 feet near what is today Highway 1, and slopes down through the central portion of the reserve. The lowest and most recent of the old marine terraces emerged about 10,000 years ago and sits at an elevation of about 40 feet above the current sea level. The short descent along the road to Whalers Cove marks this ancient shoreline.

Around 6,000 years ago, the ocean stabilized at its current level and began its assault on the shoreline. Waves chewed away at fractures and faults in the hard granodiorite to form the rugged north shore of the reserve. Headland Cove and Whalers Cove are excellent examples of how pounding waves have exploited weakness in the granodiorite, while in the process creating some of the most scenic coastline in the world. At the south end of the reserve, beautiful white sand beaches have formed at China Cove and Gibson Beach, composed of mineral grains eroded from the surrounding granodiorite.

The story written in the rocks of Point Lobos reveals an ancient and dynamic cycle of change resulting from some of the most powerful forces of nature. It is easy to assume that what we now experience has been here forever and will always stay this way, but if we take the past as our guide, it is likely that Point Lobos will again slip into the sea. With that in mind, we are fortunate to experience this grand landscape as it currently exists.

wildlife

One of the most outstanding features of Point Lobos is the diversity of wildlife thriving both on land and in the marine reserve. This is largely due to a wide variety of habitats, including cypress and pine forests, mixed woodlands, meadows, coastal scrub, rocky islands and the ocean shore. Underwater, the mammals, fish, and invertebrates flourishing in the marine reserve represent a healthy cross-section of marine animals found between southern California and the Gulf of Alaska. Point Lobos is also one of the best places along the coast of California for viewing sea birds and marine mammals such as whales and sea otters.

Mammals

Of the approximately 20 land mammals living at Point Lobos, the most commonly seen are ground squirrels, gray squirrels, black-tailed

Ground squirrel. Photo: Jeff Thomson

deer and brush rabbits. Ground squirrels, probably the most noticeable mammals at the reserve, are usually found burrowing in well-drained soil near the shoreline and in the coastal scrub plants. They are very sociable animals and can often be seen begging visitors for a snack, especially near the parking area at Sea Lion Point. (Please resist the temptation to feed them. Not only is it against the rules but it is possibly dangerous for you, since they may bite.) As the small mammals and deer have increased in population, so have their predators. Coyotes, gray foxes, badgers, bobcats and mountain lions have been sighted in the reserve. Also present is the long-tailed weasel. A relative of the sea otter, these aggressive little animals are extremely efficient hunters and have been known to take on animals many times their size, although they usually feed on mice and gophers.

Rarely seen are the more elusive nocturnal mammals, including raccoons, opossums, and skunks, whose tracks in the sand or dirt are often the only indication of their presence. One interesting nocturnal mammal is the dusky-footed wood rat. This compulsive collector is more commonly called a "pack rat" for its tendency to gather shiny objects like tin foil, buttons and coins. While you probably will not see a wood rat during the day, you might find their stick pile nests near trails that travel through the cypress, pine and oak forests.

Reptiles and Amphibians

Amphibians, the first vertebrate animals to brave the demands of life out of water, include frogs, salamanders and toads. Since their skin is not watertight, amphibians have never been able to separate themselves fully from a wet or moist environment. They can usually be found near a reliable source of fresh water and in cool, dark and damp places under rocks or logs and in moist tree hollows. Point Lobos is home to the California slender salamander, Oregon salamander, arboreal salamander, California newt and the Pacific treefrog, probably the most numerous amphibian at the reserve. The Pacific treefrog is active at all times of day and, despite its name, lives on the ground in grass and shrubs. It can be identified by a black stripe that runs across its eye and by a high-pitched croak which has been used in countless movies by Hollywood film makers.

Reptiles, which evolved from amphibians, solved the problem of water loss in part by developing a dry and scaly skin which enables them to survive in dry conditions. There are two groups of reptiles at Point Lobos: lizards and snakes. Lizards you may see at the reserve include the alligator lizard, western fence lizard and western skink. As its name implies, the alligator lizard resembles a miniature alligator, but at a length of only 12 inches, it is nothing to fear. They are most often observed sunning themselves on rock outcroppings along the trails. The western fence lizard is usually only briefly glimpsed while scurrying for cover or doing "push-ups" as a territorial gesture.

While hiking around the reserve, you may encounter an occasional snake. Those you see are harmless and include the garter snake, rubber boa, ringneck snake and two types of racer snakes. So far, no poisonous snakes have been seen at Point Lobos.

Birds

Over 200 bird species have been observed at Point Lobos, 50 of which live at the reserve year-round. (Serious birders can find a bird checklist available at the Information Station.) The wide variety of birds found here is due to the reserve's location between two overlapping life zones, the ocean's influence and the diversity of habitats found within a relatively small area. Birds are most abundant from September through the spring months when you can see many pelagic (ocean) birds nesting on nearby islands. Wintering birds include Brandt's cormorants, brown pelicans, grebes, murres and auklets.

Great blue heron. Photo: Jeff Thomson

With luck, some of the land birds you might see are iridescent hummingbirds, rock and mourning doves, groups of California quail bustling through the underbrush, dark-eyed juncos, white-crowned sparrows, hairy woodpeckers, scrub jays, plus northern flickers, which are easily identified by their black necklace and black-spotted belly. Also, look for pigmy nuthatches working their way down a tree trunk while brown creepers spiral up the trunk, both searching for insects in the bark. A fairly recent addition to the bird population at Point Lobos is the wild turkey. It feeds and nests on the ground and can occasionally be seen roosting on tree limbs in the mixed pine and oak forests. Predatory birds at Point Lobos include peregrine falcons, red-tailed and sharp-shinned hawks, barn owls and American kestrels.

About a third of the bird species found at Point Lobos are here as a result of the ocean's influence. Along the shore, look for the American black oystercatcher with its distinctive bright red bill, red eyes, black body and pink legs. During the fall and winter months you may see black turnstones which, as their name implies, use their bill to turn over small rocks and pebbles in search of insects and invertebrates. Around Whalers Cove you might spot a great blue heron. Standing up to four feet tall, these blue-gray feathered birds are graceful in flight and can sometimes be seen perched on floating driftwood and kelp waiting for their next meal to swim by. Another tall bird you may see feeding along the shoreline is the great egret. This all-white bird resembles the great blue heron in shape and size and can be further identified by its long black legs and yellow beak. The robin-sized killdeer is an interesting bird that also feeds along the seashore. When their nest is threatened by a predator, killdeers create a distraction by dragging themselves across the ground feigning a broken wing. A common killdeer nesting area is the southwest portion of Mound Meadow.

The largest sea bird at Point Lobos is the brown pelican, which can be seen from spring to fall perched on Bird Island or flying close to the ocean shore. When feeding, brown pelicans dive into the water and scoop fish into their sizable bill pouch. Two types of cormorants can be seen at Point Lobos: Brandt's and pelagic. The Brandt's cormorant is more numerous and larger than the pelagic cormorant, although most visitors will have difficulty telling the two apart. Brandt's cormorants perch and nest in large groups on Bird Island and Guillemot Island, while pelagic cormorants prefer to nest in small hollows or depressions along the face of cliffs. While feeding, both dive and swim underwater using their legs for propulsion. Another diving bird found at the reserve is the pigeon guillemot. Instead of using its legs to swim, this bird actually flies underwater using its wings for propulsion. Pigeon guillemots spend most of their life on the open sea but visit the reserve in summer to nest in small cavities on and around Guillemot Island. These pigeon-sized birds are distinguished by a black body with a white wing patch and by their red feet.

The Marine Reserve

As you walk the trails at Point Lobos you are actually seeing only half of the reserve. Extending out from the shoreline is the Point Lobos Marine Reserve – 750 acres of astonishing underwater scenery and an incredible variety of marine life.

Green anemone. Photo: Jerry Loomis

Every year about 5,000 scuba divers slip below the water's surface at Whalers Cove to explore this underwater paradise. They descend into a fantastic landscape of sheer granite walls, flat plateaus, solitary stone pinnacles and submerged caves. Brightly colored anemones, sponges, sea stars and corals cloak the rocks in such profusion that not one inch of stone is left exposed. Rays of sunlight flicker down through the undulating canopy of the kelp forest to illuminate schools of blue and black rockfish. Occasionally, a curious harbor seal or sea lion glides by to investigate.

The diversity of animal species that flourish in the marine reserve is primarily due to location and weather. Off the coast of central California, a large zone of cold water that reaches north to the Gulf of Alaska converges with a body of warmer water which extends south to San Diego. As a result, you will find animals from both the cold and warmer water zones living here. Weather plays a supporting role in spring and summer when northwesterly winds push surface water out to sea and a broth of nutrient-rich water wells up from the cold depths of the nearby submarine canyons. These nutrients, high in nitrogen and phosphate, literally bathe the animals in food and provide the foundation of the food chain.

Marine Mammals

You do not need to be a scuba diver to see and enjoy the marine mammals at Point Lobos. Permanent residents of the marine reserve that you can see from the shore include southern sea otters, harbor seals and California sea lions. Gray whales are a common sight between December and May, and during early summer, you might see a juvenile elephant seal which has hauled itself out of the water to molt or sun on the rocks.

Possibly the most popular and certainly the most endearing animal at Point Lobos is the southern sea otter. Look for them floating "belly up" in the kelp beds where they spend much of their time. Some also have a habit of wrapping themselves in a "security blanket" of kelp while taking a nap. Feeding on marine invertebrates, sea otters actually help the kelp forest flourish by feasting on sea urchins which graze on this marine plant.

Sea otter wrapped in kelp. Photo: Chuck Bancroft

Unlike most other marine mammals, the sea otter does not have an insulating layer of fat. Instead they have thick fur that traps air bubbles next to their skin and a rapid metabolism to help them stay warm in the chilly ocean water. With a metabolic rate about two to three times higher than a land-based mammal of similar size, the adult sea otter will eat close to 25% of its body weight every day. Most otters tend to eat early in the morning and late in the afternoon, with each feeding lasting about 2-3 hours. They usually groom themselves following a meal, then rest in the kelp beds during the middle of the day in groups or "rafts" usually consisting of 2 to 12 otters.

While female sea otters can give birth any time of year, most pups are born between August and October. Weighing in at 3-5 pounds at birth, the pups have light brown fur which is very fluffy and keeps them floating like a cork on the water's surface. Their baby fur is replaced at about three months of age by adult fur which is sleek and dark brown. During the 5 to 8 month period the mother sea otter cares for her baby, the two are rarely separated and the pup spends most of its time riding on mother's belly.

Historically, the southern sea otter lived along the west coast of North America between British Columbia and Mexico. Beginning in the late 1700s, they were heavily hunted by fur traders, and by the mid-1800s, an estimated population of 16,000-20,000 sea otters had been reduced to near extinction. Then in the early 1900s, a small group of otters was found living about 15 miles south of Point Lobos. Today, their population has grown to about 2,300 and their range extends approximately 230 miles along the California coast from Ano Nuevo Point in Santa Cruz County south to Purisma Point in Santa Barbara County.

Starting about mid-December, gray whales can be seen off Point Lobos as they migrate south along the coast from their summer feeding grounds off the coast of Alaska to breeding grounds in the relatively warm water of lagoons on the west coast of Baja California, Mexico. Traveling in small groups known as pods, these 40-foot-long, graceful giants can be observed as they surface and exhale an enormous amount of warm air that quickly cools into mist called a spout. Gray whales will spout about three times, then stay submerged for approximately 3-5 minutes.

During the southward migration, the best time for whale watching is the first three weeks in January. During the northward migration, the best time to see them is between March and early May. Gray whales usually travel 1/4 to 1/2 mile off shore and are best viewed from Sea Lion Point and the rocky headlands on the Cypress Grove Trail.

Like the sea otter, the gray whale was also nearly hunted to extinction, in this case for its blubber, which was rendered into oil for use as lamp fuel. By 1900, the gray whale population was reduced to fewer than 2,000 animals, which became protected by international treaty in 1938. Since then, their population has grown to about 23,000 and they are no longer considered endangered. In fact, the gray whale has done so well it is the first species ever to be taken off the endangered species list. From 1862 to the late 1870s, Point Lobos was the site of a shore whaling station. Whale blubber was processed at Whalers Cove, where today you can visit the Whaling Station Museum to learn more about this period of Point Lobos history.

While gray whales are the most frequently seen whales here, there have also been sightings of humpback, minke, pilot and blue whales plus orca, or killer whales.

Harbor seals and California sea lions belong to an order of animals called pinnipeds, a combination of two Latin words: *pinna* for wing or fin and *pedis* meaning foot. Their wing-like flippers function as both rudders and paddles and enable them to dart through the water like streamlined torpedoes. Harbor seals swim comfortably along at a speed of about 10 miles per hour while the California sea lion can attain speeds of up to 35 miles per hour for short periods and will occasionally leap out of the water like a porpoise to pick up speed. These animals are also distinguished by their large eyes, conspicuous muzzles and pointed teeth. Both the harbor seal and sea lion tend to spend a fair amount of time each day on land and usually gather in groups. Out of the water, the sea lion is much more mobile than the harbor seal, since it has the ability to rotate both front and rear flippers, enabling it to walk while the harbor seal inches along on its belly.

The California sea lion is larger than the harbor seal, has a longer neck and small ear flaps. Male sea lions weigh between 500 and 800 pounds and comprise most of the population at Point Lobos. The sexually mature males leave here in June and July to join breeding females in the Channel Islands and areas further south, then return in

California sea lion. Photo: Jeff Thomson

August. Inquisitive and gregarious by nature, California sea lions often visit boats and playfully circle scuba divers and snorkelers. Their trait of almost incessant barking inspired early Spanish explorers to call this place Punta de los Lobos Marinos, Point of the Sea Wolves.

The harbor seal lives here year-round and can be distinguished from the sea lion by its smaller size, shorter neck and lack of ear flaps. Shaped like a giant sausage, the harbor seal's fur is usually spotted and because of this, it is sometimes referred to as a leopard seal. The best sites to view them are the north side of Headland Cove and Moss Cove, where they can often be seen sunning themselves on the beach or nearby rocky

Harbor seal. Photo: Jeff Thomson

islands. Male harbor seals are 5-6 feet long and weigh 250-300 pounds while the females are slightly smaller. Between April and August, pups are born on shore or sometimes in the ocean, and can swim almost from birth. Their mothers will often leave them on the beach to go fishing, so do not be alarmed if you see a baby seal by itself. Harbor seals also tend to gather in smaller groups than the sea lions and typically bask on rocks near the water line so they can make a fast get-away if frightened. One interesting behavior is their ability to sleep with their bodies almost totally submerged in the water with only the tip of their nose exposed. This behavior is called "bottling", since their nose-top resembles the mouth of a bottle floating in the water.

Life on the seashore

The picturesque coastline of Point Lobos, which lures visitors from all over the world for its scenic beauty, also teems with a variety of life between the tides. The narrow band of rocky shore that is alternately covered in water and exposed to air by the rhythm of the tides is called the intertidal zone. Between the uppermost wave-splashed rocks and the lowest shoreline, live plants and animals that have adapted to an environment which includes both pounding waves and drying winds. For the most part, life between the tides is dominated by invertebrates, animals without a backbone, such as crabs, sea stars, sea urchins and a wide variety of snails.

In the splash zone just above high tide, the surf provides moisture but no continuous cover. As a result, the animals in this area tend to be relatively few and on the small side. Acorn barnacles are a common sight, as well as periwinkles, which hide in damp crevices in the rocks.

When the tide recedes, leaving them high and dry, periwinkles will anchor themselves to a rock by secreting a drop of glue, then withdraw into their shells to await the next high tide.

In the high-tide zone, acorn barnacles and periwinkles thrive, as do limpets. Limpets are snails that have cup-shaped shells which hold a reservoir of water to help them survive dry periods. Older and larger limpets tend to live in the higher and drier tidal zones, but some will follow the receding tide by crawling down the rocks. Some maintain

A cluster of limpets. Photo: Jeff Thomson

Mussels exposed at low tide.

Photo:
Jeff Thomson

small "gardens" of algae, like the owl limpet, which shoves its shell against intruders which get too close to its garden. Two other commonly-seen invertebrates that live in the high-tide zone are black turban snails and shore crabs. When the tide ebbs, look for shore crabs dancing across the rocks in search of a meal of dead animals and plants.

As the ocean recedes further to reveal the mid-tide zone, look for giant green anemones, mussels, abalone, goose barnacles, hermit crabs and bat stars. You may also find multicolored chitons, black abalone and black turban snails, which can live as long as 30 years. One of the more interesting characters which inhabit tide pools in the mid-and high-tide zones is the hermit crab. Inquisitive and pugnacious, they do not grow a shell of their own, but instead wear the old shells of dead periwinkles or turban snails.

During the lowest tides, which occur only once or twice a month, the richest variety of plant and animal life is briefly revealed. The rocks are cloaked with a slippery covering of algae including surfgrass, feather boa kelp and sea grapes. Colorful animals in all shades of the rainbow are exposed to view, including yellow sponges, black and red abalone, multicolored sea slugs and purple sunflower stars with up to 24 arms. One interesting character on this short list of tidepool animals is the decorator crab. It makes a camouflage by taking small bits of moss, animals and algae, which it then attaches to tiny hooks on top of its shell.

The best places to find and explore tide pools at Point Lobos are along the southern shore of the reserve and at Sea Lion Point. Please be careful not to harm the animals. Be attentive to where you are stepping, both for your own safety and to spare the marine life

*Tidepools
along the
reserve's
south shore.*

Photo:
Jeff Thomson

underfoot. If you turn over a rock to examine the life growing on its
underside, return it to the place and position in which you found it.
The animals living on the bottom of the rock will die if left exposed to
the sun and air. The marine reserve was created to protect the sea life
within its boundary, so please remember that it is against the law to
collect any plants or animals.

Fish

Except for scuba divers, most visitors to Point Lobos will not be able
to enjoy the colorful variety of fish living in the marine reserve.
However, if you are a tidepool explorer, you may see sculpins, which
have developed mottled colors to match their surroundings, and
clingfish, which cling to rocks using pelvic fins converted into a sucker.
In narrow places between rocks, you might also see a slender rock-
weed gunnel with only its head sticking out.

Scuba divers may see lingcod, which hide in the stone crevices of
Bluefish Cove, as well as reef-dwelling cabezon. The short list of other
fish divers might encounter includes surf perch, a variety of rockfish,
kelp greenlings, sheepshead fish and timid leopard sharks. There have
also been infrequent sightings of great white sharks.

A word of caution: It is often dangerous to be on the shoreline, especially at high tide or when the sea is churned by waves. Even when
the sea looks calm, large unexpected waves can occur and wash people
off the rocks, so never turn your back on the ocean. Uneven and slippery rock surfaces also present a hazard.

trees & plants

Point Lobos State Reserve was created, in part, to protect what is perhaps its most enduring symbol and celebrated tree, the Monterey cypress. Now classified as a rare and endangered species, the Monterey cypress grows naturally at only two locations on earth: here at Point Lobos, and at Cypress Point on the north side of Carmel Bay. The reserve also provides refuge for approximately 350 species of flowering trees, shrubs and plants, many of which remain green year-round, the result of mild winters and cool, often foggy, summers.

Point Lobos is remarkable not just for the number of different species found within a relatively small area but also for an unusual variety of plant communities. Some have distinct borders, like the underwater kelp forest, but on land many of the trees, shrubs and plants have adapted to more than one zone. The mosaic of plant communities found here include the Monterey cypress forest, Monterey pine forest, northern coastal prairie, northern coastal scrub and the kelp forest of the marine reserve.

The Monterey Cypress Forest

Millions of years ago, vast tracts of Monterey cypress trees covered a large area along the west coast of what is now California. Because of changes in climate and geography, native stands of this tree have been reduced to the groves at Point Lobos and Cypress Point in Pebble Beach.

The last native groves of Monterey cypress survive near the face of granite headlands and within the reach of spray from crashing ocean waves. Buffeted by onshore winds, most of the trees growing along the seaward side of the groves are sculptured into twisted, flat-topped shapes that express the story of their life on the edge of the continent. An excellent example of this relationship with wind and sea is the "Old Veteran" tree located close to the North Shore Trail at Cypress Cove. Almost alone on the side of a steep cliff, its curved and flowing roots and trunk recline against the rocky hillside, giving but not breaking in its struggle with the elements. Just back from the cliff's edge, trees that are protected from the wind grow in a more symmetrical form and have a conical crown.

The Monterey cypress can be recognized by small walnut-sized round cones and tiny scale-like leaves that minimize moisture loss by reducing the surface area exposed to drying winds. In addition to the main groves near the ocean's edge, a number of cypress trees are scattered around the interior of the reserve. Several picturesque trees surround the Whalers Cabin and a few others grow near the Information Station located at the Cypress Grove Trailhead.

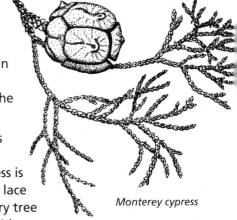

Monterey cypress

As you walk through the cypress groves, the sense of traveling through an untouched wilderness is enhanced by veils of gray-green lace lichen hanging from almost every tree branch. While often confused with Spanish moss, lichen is actually a combination of a fungus and an algae. The fungus part of the lichen builds an interlaced web which absorbs moisture from the air, while the algae, containing chlorophyll, produces food that both use for energy. Lace lichen is not limited to the cypress groves and is found growing on Monterey pine and coast live oak trees throughout the reserve. An especially pleasing visual effect is created shortly before sunset when horizontal shafts of light accentuate the filigreed lace.

Other plants you may see in the Monterey cypress groves include seaside daisy, cliff lettuce, sticky monkey flower, California sagebrush and Douglas iris, which heralds the coming of spring with its purple, cream and yellow-striped flowers. Iris is the Greek word for rainbow and refers to the alternate bands of color on this attractive flower. The Douglas iris blooms during February and March and can usually be found growing in warm pockets of the cypress groves and in other forested areas of the reserve.

The Monterey Pine Forest

Much like the Monterey cypress, native stands of Monterey pine occur only at a few places on the central coast of California, one of which is Point Lobos. While somewhat uncommon in California, the Monterey pine is probably the most commercially planted tree in the southern hemisphere, where it is prized as a timber species. Here at Point Lobos, this tree is widely distributed. In addition to pure stands in the central portion of the reserve, it forms a mixed forest with Monterey cypress near Big Dome, and blends with coast live oak trees inland.

Monterey pines grow rapidly to full size and prefer coarse, well drained soil. They can be recognized by usually straight trunks with thick, furrowed bark and by shiny green needles which develop in groups of three. Outside of the dense groves, single mature trees can develop massive, often irregular trunks with thick branches and a somewhat rounded crown. Monterey pines also grow best within the fog belt, a zone of fog that occurs along the California coast between June and August but which rarely extends very far inland. During the dry but often foggy summer months, water condenses on the pine needles and drops to the ground, providing moisture not otherwise available.

While the Monterey pine grows quickly, its life expectancy of about 100 years is relatively short compared to other trees. In order to reproduce, its cones need the heat of an unusually hot summer day or fire to open and release their seeds. On those rare days in summer when the temperature rises above 80 degrees F, so many cones may be opening that a whole tree can be heard snapping and crackling. The Monterey pine cones are also an important source

Monterey pine

of food for squirrels, which, by eating the seeds, keep young trees from growing too thickly. Also, as they carry seeds or cones about the reserve, squirrels help spread the tree to new areas.

The coast live oak tree mixes with the Monterey pine mainly in the northern and eastern areas of the reserve. It is characterized by a relatively short but sturdy trunk, crooked branches and a spreading crown of dark green, somewhat oblong leaves with needle-like teeth along their edges. With ample light and space, this tree can grow to a height of up to 80 feet. One interesting aspect of the coast live oak is that it supports a greater variety of

Coast live oak

wildlife than any other tree in the area. It is a source of food for deer, woodpeckers, squirrels, quail, and a relatively recent addition to the reserve, the wild turkey.

Plants that commonly grow in the mixed pine and oak forests include Douglas iris, sticky monkey flower, honeysuckle, bracken fern, coffeeberry, wild lilac, hedge nettle, yerba buena, wild rose and poison oak. The wild lilac or California lilac is actually a shrub and one of the more common plants in this community. Beginning in March, fragrant blue flower clusters form at the end of its woody stems. The wild rose usually blooms in May, with pink flowers that quickly fade and fall off, leaving a seed pod which turns bright red in September.

Wild lilac

During the rainy season, an incredible variety of mushrooms emerge from the forest floor or sprout on rotting logs. Fungus fanciers will find a multitude of mushrooms in almost every imaginable shape, size and color. A few of the more easily recognized mushrooms found at the reserve are *Amanita muscaria* with its bright red cap, *Sparassis crispa* and pumpkin-colored *Gymnopilus spectabilis* which grows in large clusters at the base of dead or dying pine trees. One type of fungus, pitch canker, was introduced into central California in 1986 and poses a serious threat to Monterey pine trees. Signs of an infected tree include needles that fade from dark green to brown and pitchy cankers that develop on all woody parts of the tree.

Northern Coastal Prairie

Throughout the year, the meadows of Point Lobos provide visitors with a constantly changing mosaic of color: vibrant shades of gold, yellow, blue and red in spring, splashes of red, yellow and burgundy in summer, followed by the browns and greens of fall and winter. Northern coastal prairie flora occur at Mound Meadow, Carmelo Meadow and in the grasslands of the northern portion of the reserve. These meadows are considered to be the southern limit of northern coastal prairie habitat.

The coastal prairies at Mound Meadow and Carmelo Meadow are dominated by tall and dense-growing annual grasses. Most of the native grasses in California are perennials that have deep roots, live for several years and grow in clumps. Most of the annual grasses here are non-native species which sprout with the winter rains and finish their flowering and seeding before the soil dries. Non-native grasses from the Mediterranean region were introduced to this area by early Spanish explorers and settlers whose cattle probably grazed nearby as early as the 1840s. The spread of non-native plants at Point Lobos was hastened when Carmelo Meadow was cultivated with garden crops, beginning in the early 1860s. In order to foster a return of native plant communities, some areas of the reserve, including the meadows, are occasionally burned by the park service using controlled fires to limit the spread of intruding trees, shrubs and plants. Nutrients in the resulting ash also serve as fertilizer during the spring growth period.

At Mound Meadow you can find several species of grasses, including the native giant wild rye, whose seeds were used as a food source by the indigenous people of this area, and the non-native little rattlesnake grass, which has a flower pod that resembles the end of a rattlesnake tail. Other flowering plants at Mound Meadow include footsteps-of-spring, sea pink and star tulips. The sea pink grows best within 100 yards of the ocean. It has grassy leaves and usually blooms between March and April with round balls of pink blossoms. In early March look for the golden-flowered footsteps-of-spring, then from May to June the star tulip, with its large pinkish-white flowers. At Carmelo Meadow on Whalers Cove, you will also find many of the grasses and flowering plants that occur at Mound Meadow plus grass iris, which is often referred to as blue-eyed grass. From late March through June it forms an attractive purple carpet around moist areas in the meadow.

In the meadow that extends from the reserve's northern boundary down to Granite Point, you can find yellow California buttercups which bloom in late February, and California poppies that begin their grand display in March. Another yellow flower which thrives in this meadow is the sun cup. Look for it along the Moss Cove Trail beginning in late February. Depending on the time of year, you may also see expanses of field mustard and pockets of wild rose.

California poppy

Fresh water seeps to the surface in two narrow corridors of the northern meadow and supports plants that depend on a high water table. Two of the more interesting flowering plants that grow here are scarlet pimpernel and sweet fennel. The non-native scarlet pimpernel is a short, creeping plant that blooms from March to May with small pinkish-orange flowers. This poisonous plant is also called poor-man's-weather-glass, since the flowers close on cloudy days, then open again when the sun comes out. Sweet fennel is a tall plant that grows 3-6 feet in height, has feathery leaves and small yellow flowers at the end of its branches. All parts of this plant are edible and produce a mild licorice flavor. As a word of caution, sweet fennel resembles poison hemlock, all parts of which are poisonous if ingested. Sedges and rushes also grow in places along the fresh water seeps. Generations of Native American basket weavers used sedges to create beautiful, intricately woven baskets.

The Northern Coastal Scrub Community

This plant community consists of densely growing, woody-stemmed shrubs and plants which are able to survive in what is sometimes a harsh environment. These plants generally grow on sandy and porous soil and have developed interesting ways to conserve water. To reduce evaporation, some have small leathery leaves or fine hairs on the leaves that help reduce water loss, while others reflect the sunlight with silver-gray foliage. During the dry summer months, fog produces some moisture and the gray skies keep the temperature low.

Coyote bush

The most common scrub community plants are shrubs such as the almost ever-present poison oak, coyote bush, buckwheat, wild lilac and California sagebrush. Poison oak, which borders most of the trails through this community, plays an important role in the ecosystem by stabilizing the soil and providing a home for a number of small mammals. However, many people are allergic to the oil poison oak produces on its leaves and stems, so it is wise to avoid physical contact with this plant. *(See page 39 for more information about poison oak.)*

Another common shrub is the evergreen coyote bush. Look for small glossy leaves with occasional notches along their edge. Along the fringes of the coastal scrub, wild lilac plants produce showy blue flowers in spring. Two other common flowering plants are the red seaside painted cup and the orange blossoms of the sticky monkey flower.

Coastal bluff scrub plants, a sub-community of the northern coastal scrub, occupy a narrow band of land bordering the low ocean headlands extending north from Whalers Cove and south from Sea Lion Point. This scrub vegetation is exposed to almost continuous wind, and has developed a low mat-like appearance with most of the plants rarely exceeding two feet in height. Plant species you will find in this community include seaside painted cup, cliff lettuce, seaside daisy, cat's ear (look for leaves that are hairy on both sides), sand spurry and mock heather, which sends forth clusters of small yellow flowers in August and is noteworthy as the reserve's latest-blooming wildflower.

Mock heather

The Underwater Kelp Forest

The plants that comprise the kelp forest are members of a group of plants called algae. One of the most basic of all plants, algae range in size from the microscopic to giant brown kelp, which often grow up to 100 feet long. Algae that can be seen without a microscope are called seaweeds and fall into three groups: green, red and brown.

The most noticeable plants in the underwater reserve belong to the brown algae group. The largest of the brown algae are called kelp, and include the bull kelp which is predominant in the rough waters outside of protected bays and the giant kelp, which prefers calmer water. Instead of roots, these plants anchor themselves to underwater rocks with a multibranched structure called a holdfast. Growing from the holdfast is a tough yet flexible stipe that functions like a stem to transfer food generated in the flat, leaf-like blades near the ocean surface down to the lower sections of the plant. Bull kelp has stipes

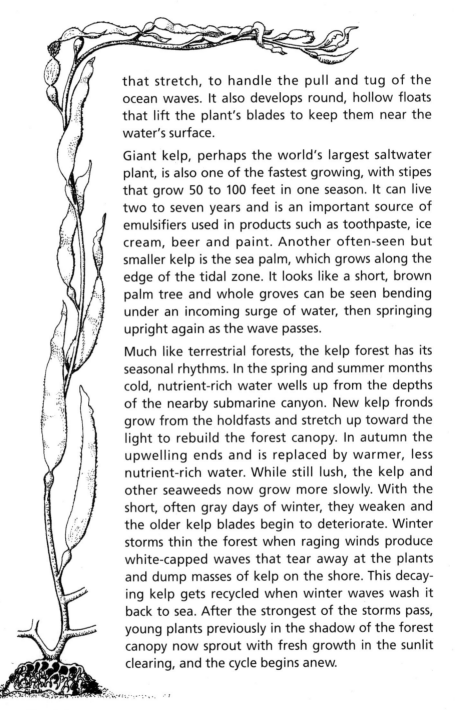

that stretch, to handle the pull and tug of the ocean waves. It also develops round, hollow floats that lift the plant's blades to keep them near the water's surface.

Giant kelp, perhaps the world's largest saltwater plant, is also one of the fastest growing, with stipes that grow 50 to 100 feet in one season. It can live two to seven years and is an important source of emulsifiers used in products such as toothpaste, ice cream, beer and paint. Another often-seen but smaller kelp is the sea palm, which grows along the edge of the tidal zone. It looks like a short, brown palm tree and whole groves can be seen bending under an incoming surge of water, then springing upright again as the wave passes.

Much like terrestrial forests, the kelp forest has its seasonal rhythms. In the spring and summer months cold, nutrient-rich water wells up from the depths of the nearby submarine canyon. New kelp fronds grow from the holdfasts and stretch up toward the light to rebuild the forest canopy. In autumn the upwelling ends and is replaced by warmer, less nutrient-rich water. While still lush, the kelp and other seaweeds now grow more slowly. With the short, often gray days of winter, they weaken and the older kelp blades begin to deteriorate. Winter storms thin the forest when raging winds produce white-capped waves that tear away at the plants and dump masses of kelp on the shore. This decaying kelp gets recycled when winter waves wash it back to sea. After the strongest of the storms pass, young plants previously in the shadow of the forest canopy now sprout with fresh growth in the sunlit clearing, and the cycle begins anew.

Giant kelp

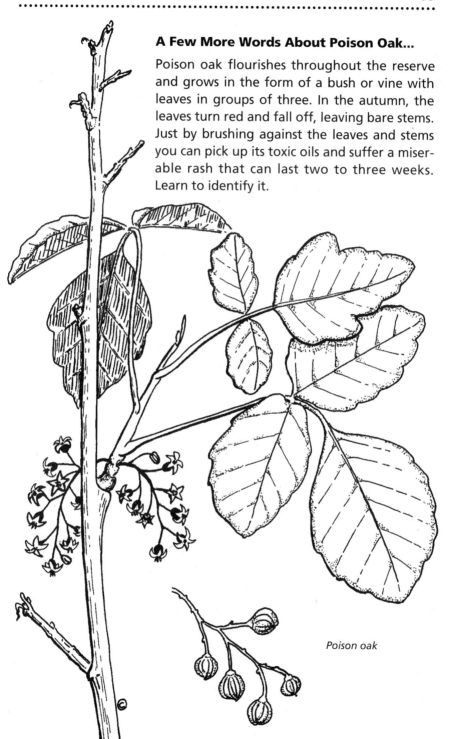

A Few More Words About Poison Oak...

Poison oak flourishes throughout the reserve and grows in the form of a bush or vine with leaves in groups of three. In the autumn, the leaves turn red and fall off, leaving bare stems. Just by brushing against the leaves and stems you can pick up its toxic oils and suffer a miserable rash that can last two to three weeks. Learn to identify it.

Poison oak

the trails

The reserve has about nine miles of trails for you to enjoy. Some trace the scenic shoreline while others explore the forests or meander along open meadows. Most of the trails are relatively short and range in difficulty from easy to moderate. Portions of the Sea Lion Point and Sand Hill Trails, which lead to spectacular ocean views, are wheelchair accessible.

Selecting Your Hike

The trails listed in this book are described according to their level of difficulty. Since you are the best judge of your physical condition, these ratings should be used as a general guide.

Easy: Uneven but fairly level.
Moderate: Some steep grades mixed with level stretches.

Please Note: Every attempt has been made to describe the trails as accurately as possible. However, natural events can significantly change trail conditions. You should not use any of the trails without acknowledging and assuming the risks involved. Please use common sense and caution. *You are responsible for determining your own physical ability and for your own safety while using the reserve's trails.*

Trail Distances
(One way unless otherwise specified)

	Miles
Bird Island Trail	0.8 round trip
Carmelo Meadow Trail	0.1
Cypress Grove Trail	0.8 round trip
Granite Point Trail	1.3
Lace Lichen Trail	0.5
Moss Cove Trail	0.6 round trip
Mound Meadow Trail	0.3
North Shore Trail	1.4
Pine Ridge Trail	0.7
Sand Hill Trail	0.2
Sea Lion Point Trail	0.6 round trip
South Plateau Trail	0.7
South Shore Trail	1.0
Whalers Cabin Trail	0.1
Whalers Knoll Trail	0.5 to traverse the knoll

Bird Island Trail

Trailhead: The Bird Island Picnic Area

Distance: 0.8 miles round trip

Classification: Easy

HIGHLIGHTS – The Bird Island Trail combines stunning coastline scenery with the opportunity to view nesting sea birds in spring and summer.

This trail begins at a spectacular cliffside overlook where ocean waves surge around offshore rocks, then crash into a picturesque cove carved from the granite headlands. On a calm day, look for sea otters in the cove's kelp forest or perhaps a harbor seal basking on a rock.

From its start, the trail makes a short climb under the shade of Monterey pine trees then levels out as it emerges from the woods, where you are presented with your first view of white-capped Bird Island. From here, your path winds along the scrub-and pine-covered hillside, then around the next turn you come upon China Cove with its beautiful emerald-green waters and white sand beach. China Cove and nearby Gibson Beach are the only two places at the reserve where swimming is allowed, but be forewarned, the water is cold, even in summer.

From the stairway that leads down to China Cove, your trail bends to the left and quickly arrives at a trail junction overlooking crescent-shaped Gibson Beach and the Carmel Highlands area. The sparkling white sands of Gibson Beach

China Cove.   Photo: Jeff Thomson

and China Cove are composed of small grains of white feldspar and gray quartz which have eroded from the granite-like rock that surrounds these coves. If you want to explore Gibson Beach, turn to the left and in a few yards you will find a sign pointing to the stairs that descend to the beach. Gibson Creek, which flows into the ocean at the south end of the beach, forms the reserve's southern boundary.

Gibson Beach looks the same today as it did in this photo taken in 1929 during the filming of Evangeline.

Photo: Pat Hathaway Photo Collection

The Bird Island Trail continues to the right from the trail junction and winds along the hillside through a dense growth of coastal scrub plants. During the summer months, these plants put on a showy display of white, gold, yellow and orange flowers. Just ahead, the path arrives at flat-topped Pelican Point and begins a counter-clockwise loop around the point. Almost immediately, you pass above a narrow chasm formed by ocean waves eating away at a fracture in the hard granodiorite rock. The overall effect is quite impressive and underscores the power of ocean waves which, during periods of heavy surf, exert tons of force as they thunder ashore.

As you come around to the west side of the point, Bird Island is now in close view. During the spring and early summer months, this island is a nesting site for large colonies of Brandt's cormorants. Their nests, made of seaweed gathered by the male bird, are packed close together along the island's high ridge and steep slopes. Nesting activity takes place between May and June with the chicks hatching in late June. Less easily seen are pelagic cormorants which nest in cavities along the side of sheer cliffs and offshore rocks. They are somewhat smaller than Brandt's cormorants and during the breeding season can be distinguished by a patch of white on their sides. The spring months are also a good time to observe black-crowned night herons nesting on rocky ledges on the small island between the trail and Bird Island. These stocky birds can be identified by a cap of black head feathers, black back and long white breeding plumes which are displayed as a greeting gesture.

Another sea bird commonly seen here between spring and fall is the brown pelican. As recently as the 1930s, up to 3,000 of these large birds gathered here to nest on Bird Island, but in the mid-1960s, their numbers were significantly reduced. By the 1970s, this species was threatened by extinction because of DDT they absorbed from their fish diet. Since the use of DDT was banned, the brown pelican population has rebounded. However, they have not yet begun to nest again on Bird Island and are still on the federal list of endangered birds. In addition to sightings on Bird Island, brown pelicans can often be seen flying along the shoreline in single-line or V formations.

A western gull mother standing over her nest and eggs. Photo: Jeff Thomson

The western gull, a permanent resident at the reserve, nests on the rocky slopes of Bird Island as well as in other areas along the shoreline. By late spring, they have established their nests, occasionally only inches from a well-traveled trail. Around mid-to-late June, the chicks hatch and stay in their nests for another five to seven weeks. During this period, the parents may become aggressive with humans if they feel threatened. When the parents sense danger, they give a signal to the chicks, which instantly hide or stop moving.

As the trail turns away from Bird Island, the dramatic seascape is enhanced by chasms, arches and sea caves reflecting this battleground between surf and shore.

Carmelo Meadow Trail

Trailhead: The entrance station

Distance: 0.1 miles

Classification: Easy

HIGHLIGHTS – This trail provides a short connection between the entrance station and Whalers Cove area.

About 10 yards past the entrance station, turn right at a sign announcing the Carmelo Meadow Trail. From the trailhead, you will descend into a forest of Monterey pine and coast live oak trees. Old photos show this area as almost devoid of trees, but around the mid- to late-1930s, Monterey pines began to spread into the upper meadow from nearby groves. While the Monterey pine grows quickly, its life expectancy of about 100 years is relatively short compared to other trees. In order to reproduce, its cones need the heat from a fire or an unusually hot day to open and release their seeds. A controlled burn of this area in 1993 allowed many cones to open, so most of the young trees you see date back to that time.

The trail levels out as you leave the forest, then winds along the edge of the open meadow. Carmelo Meadow supports a number of sedges and grasses native to California as well as many non-native plants introduced by early settlers. The meadow plants provide habitat for a number of small birds and mammals who attract hawks and owls as well as coyotes, bobcats and badgers.

For almost 150 years Carmelo Meadow and Whalers Cove were the center of most commercial activity at Point Lobos. Starting in the early 1850s, a small Chinese fishing village was established on the south side of Whalers Cove. Then in 1862, Portuguese whalers and their families arrived and settled in Carmelo Meadow. Reports from that era describe their tidy whitewashed cottages and gardens. Carmelo Meadow was also the site of a proposed housing subdivision which was laid out in 1890. The development was originally named Point Lobos City but soon became known as Carmelito, and consisted of

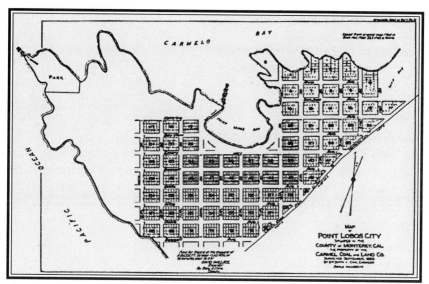

Plot map of Carmelito

almost 1,000 lots, quite a few of which were sold. Fortunately, the town never became a reality, due in large part to the efforts of A. M. Allan in the late 1890s. Allan, who gained financial control of the development company, then set about buying back the lots that had already been sold. About thirty years later, the State of California purchased 348 acres of property at Point Lobos from the Allan family to establish the reserve.

The Carmelo Meadow Trail comes to an end where it meets the Granite Point Trail on the bluff above Whalers Cove. A left turn on the Granite Point Trail leads to the Whalers Cabin and Whaling Station Museums while a right turn will take you over to Coal Chute Point, Granite Point and the Moss Cove Trail.

Cypress Grove Trail

Trailhead: The Information Station at the Sea Lion Point Parking Area

Distance: 0.8 miles

Classification: Easy

HIGHLIGHTS – As the name implies, this short loop trail travels through a beautiful Monterey cypress forest. Along the way, you will enjoy spectacular views of ocean waves surging against the rocky headlands, picturesque coves and excellent whale watching during the annual winter gray whale migration. Bring your camera and binoculars!

From the signed trailhead next to the Information Station, your path leads through a coastal scrub plant community dominated by densely-growing woody-stemmed shrubs. This section of the trail is bordered by a nearly impenetrable wall of poison oak (do not touch), giant rye, coyote bush, buckwheat and California sagebrush, along with

Hedge nettle

other seasonally flowering plants including hedge nettle, and sticky monkey flower with its trumpet-shaped orange blossoms. Also, look for ground squirrels and brush rabbits scurrying along the path.

After walking a short distance you will reach the Monterey cypress forest and a sign announcing the Allan Memorial Grove. This grove of rare and endangered native trees was preserved by A. M. Allan, who in the late 1890s purchased most of the land now within the reserve from the Carmelo Land and Coal Company, which had subdivided the area around Whaler's Cove for a real estate development. When the Allan family heirs sold a portion of their land at Point Lobos to the California State Parks in 1933, they also donated this 15 acre cypress grove in memory of A. M. Allan and his wife, Satie.

To continue on, turn left at the Memorial Grove sign. The trail briefly travels through the forest shade, then soon comes to an open area along the cliff that affords an excellent view of Headland Cove. Look for harbor seals basking on the shore or perhaps a sea otter floating in the kelp beds. Just a short distance further, you will come to a pile of rounded granodiorite boulders. If you stop a few yards in front of the boulders and look to the right you will find a 3 to 4 foot tall pile of sticks, home to a dusky-footed wood rat. These compulsive collectors are especially attracted to shiny objects like buttons and coins, which they carry back to their nest. Wood rats or pack rats, as they are often called, are common at the reserve but seldom seen, since they rarely come out during the day.

Past the boulders, the trail soon returns to the forest and climbs to a vista point overlooking Sea Lion Rocks and the churning waters of Devil's Cauldron. On a clear day, the view south extends over 15 miles down the majestic Big Sur coast. If you look closely, you might be able to see a flicker of light from the lighthouse on dome-shaped Point Sur looming in the distance.

Proceeding ahead, you will quickly arrive at South Point, a rocky promontory located on top of a steep granite cliff. Below your feet, seawater surges over and through narrow rocky chasms and occasionally bursts upon the headland with enough force to send a light spray over the trail. To your right a jagged finger of rock called the Pinnacle

juts out from the headland. While it may look like a slender peninsula, the Pinnacle is actually an island, one of 464 islands, some only the size of your hand, that line the shore of the reserve.

In addition to its scenic beauty, South Point is also a popular place to view marine wildlife. Starting around mid-December, gray whales can be seen about a half-mile off the coast as they migrate south from their feeding grounds off the coast of Alaska to breeding grounds in the relatively warm water of lagoons on the west coast of Baja California, Mexico. During the southward migration, the best time for whale

The Pinnacle. Photo: Jeff Thomson

watching is the first three weeks of January. During the northward migration, the best time to see this amazing parade is between March and early May. If you are visiting during the spring or summer months, look for pelagic cormorants nesting in small hollows along the face of perpendicular cliffs and Brandt's cormorants, which are occasionally seen perched on the Pinnacle. Both of these birds feed by diving into the ocean and swimming after fish.

Leaving South Point the trail scrambles down the rocks, turns a corner and descends a series of granite steps. After you reach the bottom of the steps take a look to your right to view an attractive cascade of bluff lettuce growing in the crevices of a sheer granite wall. The trail soon levels out and winds along the cliff through a fantastic scene of twisted cypress trees whose limbs are draped with webs of lace lichen and covered with an orange-red algae. The gray-green lichen is an excellent example of a rela-tionship between a fungus and an algae, where both partners benefit. The fungus part of the lichen builds the interlaced web which absorbs moisture from the air while the algae, which contains chlorophyll, produces food which both use for energy. *Trentepohlia,* the rust-colored algae that covers the lower branches of the cypress trees, is actually a green algae which contains a carotene pigment that masks the green chlorophyll. Both the lace lichen and *trentepohlia* algae are harmless to the trees.

Bluff lettuce

After winding a short distance through the forest, the trail comes to a wood bench where a short spur trail leads left to an overlook at North Point. From this viewpoint, you can gaze over Carmel Bay to the white sands of Carmel Beach and the green fairways of the golf course at Pebble Beach. Below the water's surface, the Carmel Submarine Canyon begins just off the shoreline and reaches a depth of 1,200 feet where it meets the Monterey Submarine Canyon in the Monterey Bay Marine Sanctuary. Starting during the spring months and continuing through summer, cold water wells up from the canyon depths and provides nutrients for the underwater life. This phenomenon is also partially responsible for the foggy summers along the central coast of California. As warm air passes over the cold surface water of the ocean, it condenses to form fog, which the onshore sea breeze pushes against the coast.

Just below the rocks of North Point, you may notice shell fragments along the path. These were left by the Ohlone, the indigenous people of this area, who occupied this site while gathering shellfish. The shell fragments are part of what is essentially a pre-historic trash heap that anthropologists call a midden.

From the wood bench, your path descends about 50 yards to another spur trail on the left that leads down to a cliffside vista overlooking Cypress Cove. In the water below, you may observe sea otters drifting in the kelp or catch a glimpse of an American black oystercatcher flying low across the water. Its black feathers blend well against the dark, algae-covered rocks, but it can be identified by a bright red bill and pink legs. This vocal shorebird does not feed on oysters as its name implies, but on limpets which it pries off rocks with its strong bill.

Back on the main trail, you will soon leave the forest and return to the coastal scrub, then complete the loop as you pass by the Allan Memorial Grove sign. On your way back to the trailhead, you can take a short detour to see the Old Veteran Cypress by turning left on the North Shore Trail. When you reach the Old Veteran sign, go left on the spur trail to see the elegant roots, trunk and canopy of this magnificent tree.

The mouth of Cypress Cove. Photo: Jeff Thomson

Granite Point Trail

Trailhead: Across the road from Whalers Cabin
at Whalers Cove

Distance: 1.3 miles round trip

Classification: Easy

HIGHLIGHTS – In addition to its exceptional scenic value, the Granite Point Trail travels through an area rich in human history.

Your path begins across from the Whalers Cabin, the only structure that remains from a small Chinese fishing village established in the early 1850s. Whalers Cove has also been the site of a granite quarry, whaling station, abalone cannery, gravel quarry, coal shipping station and during World War II, various military operations. In the 1890s, the meadow above the cove was slated for development as a residential subdivision that fortunately never materialized.

Along most of its length, the Granite Point Trail is bordered by a narrow band of coastal scrub vegetation. Most of these plants grow very close to the ground and have adapted to an environment of shallow soil, frequent winds and salt spray from crashing waves. In late spring and early summer, many of them bloom to make the water's edge one of the most colorful places in the reserve. Look for the lavender flowers of seaside daisies, yellow dwarf brodiaeas, red seaside painted cups, and gold California poppies.

Seaside daisy

About mid-way around Whalers Cove, the Granite Point Trail meets the Carmelo Meadow Trail, which comes in from the right. Here you will find a bench where you can pause and gaze over the cove. Look for sea otters floating in the kelp and harbor seals "bottling" in the cove or sunning themselves on nearby rocks. You might even spot a snowy egret or its larger cousin, the great blue heron, standing motionless near the shore or perched on a piece of floating driftwood waiting for a passing fish.

Continuing on, your path enters a forest of Monterey pine trees and is lined by a thick understory of wild blackberry and poison oak. As you leave the woods, the trail turns to the left and stays close to the cliff above several offshore rocks favored by harbor seals. A short distance further, the trail arrives at the site of Kodani Village.

In 1896, a young marine biologist from Japan, Gennosuke Kodani, arrived at Point Lobos and soon established a commercial abalone-harvesting business. He employed divers from his native village of Chiba, who used bulky hard-hat diving suits, one of which is on display in the Whalers Cabin. At first, the abalone they gathered were dried on wooden racks that extended along Coal Chute Point. Then, in the late 1890s, Kodani formed a partnership with Alexander Allan, who had recently purchased the property that now forms the reserve. They built an

Gennosuke Kodani.
Courtesy: Seizo Kodani Family

Japanese village c. 1926. *Courtesy: Seizo Kodani Family*

abalone cannery that operated until 1928, located at what is now the Whalers Cove Parking Area. Kodani and his wife, Fuku Tahiro, raised nine children, eight of whom were born in the family home located here on the north side of the cove. While nothing remains of the Kodani home or those of the abalone divers who settled along this section of the trail, the naming of Kodani Village is tribute to the man who pioneered the modern abalone fishing industry.

Just past the Kodani Village site you will come to a fork in the trail. Stay to the left where the trail forms a Y and trace the path of an old ore cart tramway out to Coal Chute Point. In the mid-1870s, low grade coal was discovered in a canyon a short distance southeast of here. After being mined, the coal was transported by horse-drawn wagons to a short tramway that began east of what is now Highway 1. There it was loaded into ore carts, which were pulled along the tramway to a coal chute constructed on the point. The coal mine operated until the late 1890s, when it closed because of high operating costs and poor market conditions.

Out on Coal Chute Point, you have an excellent view across the opening of Whalers Cove to Cannery Point and tree-covered headlands in the distance. From here, the trail heads inland along the edge of the point above Coal Chute Cove, then climbs through a patch of giant wild rye and a profusion of seaside daisy plants which bloom in early spring and display their lavender-colored flowers into autumn. In short order, you complete the loop and arrive at a bench overlooking a small gravel-covered beach known as the Pit. Back in the 1920s, this beach was the site of a gravel quarry. The rocks were hauled a short distance north to what is now Monastery Beach where they were crushed into gravel, then shipped off to market.

As the trail travels north above the wave-sculpted cove, it is lined with a hedge-like growth of coastal scrub plants dominated by poison oak. Then after a short descent, you arrive at a signpost marking the Moss Cove Trail, which heads off to the right. To your left, a short spur trail leads down through a cut in the hillside to the beach at Coal Chute Cove. The Granite Point Trail proceeds across the intersection where you have a choice of going left or right to loop around the point. For the purpose of this trail description we will turn left and head up and along the south side of Granite Point with Whalers Cove to our left.

During most of the year, the wind maintains a steady presence at Granite Point and as a result, the cliff-side vegetation grows low to the ground. Visitors to the reserve in May and June will find a multicolored carpet of wildflowers blooming in shades of orange, red, yellow, and purple. At the tip of the point, wind-or storm-driven waves often crash against the headland and surge into small coves which have developed along fractures in the hard rock. As the trail continues around the point, you have an open view of crescent-shaped Moss Cove, Hudson Meadow and the white sands of Carmel River State Beach.

As you complete the loop around Granite Point the trail returns to its intersection with the Moss Cove Trail. By turning left on this trail, you can extend your walk 0.3 miles through the meadow to the reserve's northern boundary.

Moss Cove. Photo: Jeff Thomson

Lace Lichen Trail

Trailhead: Located on the left side of the entrance road at the first intersection past the entrance station.

Distance: 0.5 miles

Classification: Easy

HIGHLIGHTS – The Lace Lichen Trail parallels the entrance road and provides hikers with a direct route from the ranger station to the Piney Woods Picnic Area.

This trail begins about 100 yards past the entrance station and across the street from the road that leads to Whalers Cove. There you will find a signpost for the Mound Meadow Trail which goes left (south) to Hidden Beach and the Lace Lichen Trail which heads to the right (west) into a forest of Monterey pine and coast live oak trees. The indigenous people of this area, the Ohlone, used acorns from the oak tree as a staple of their diet along with nuts from the Monterey pine. (To find out how the acorns were processed, see the Moss Cove Trail description.) The Ohlone also made use of another plant that is common along this trail, the sticky monkey flower. Stems and leaves from this evergreen shrub were crushed and applied to the skin to heal wounds. You can identify the sticky monkey flower by its woody stems and dark green leaves, the undersides of which are sticky to the touch, and in summer by its trumpet-shaped orange flowers.

Sticky monkey flower

The Lace Lichen Trail is named after a plant which is the combination of two organisms, a fungus and an algae, that have developed a mutually beneficial relationship. The fungus part of the plant builds an interlaced web which absorbs moisture from the air, while the algae, containing chlorophyll, produces food that both use for energy. Lace lichen is not overly abundant along this mostly sunny trail but can be seen hanging from tree branches in some of the shady areas.

Lace lichen

From its start, your path is bordered by rattlesnake grass and grass iris. Between late March and the end of June, grass iris, which is also called blue-eyed grass, sends up purple blooms on a stem about 8 inches high. You will also find a number of young Monterey pine trees which started growing after this area was burned by the rangers in 1993 as part of an ecosystem management program. These controlled fires limit the potential of a devastating wildfire by reducing the amount of dead plant material on the ground and also improve conditions for the survival of pine seedlings.

At about its halfway point, the trail bends to the left and passes through a thick stand of California lilac before emerging into the open, where sticky monkey flower plants grow in profusion. A short distance further, you will arrive at a signpost marking the west end of the Pine Ridge Trail. A left turn on the Pine Ridge Trail quickly leads to a spur trail on the right that heads down to the Piney Woods Picnic Area. From its intersection with the Pine Ridge Trail, the Lace Lichen Trail makes a gradual turn to the right and leads over to the paved entrance road where you can access the Whalers Knoll Trail, which starts on the opposite side of the road.

Moss Cove Trail

Trailhead: At the east end of the Granite Point Trail

Distance: 0.6 miles round trip

Classification: Easy

HIGHLIGHTS – The Moss Cove Trail travels through a meadow which is covered with beautiful wildflowers during the spring and summer months. At the trail's end on Ichxenta Point, there are excellent views of Carmel Bay and evidence of the earliest inhabitants of this area.

To reach Moss Cove, follow the Granite Point Trail 0.5 miles from its start across from the Whalers Cabin. When you arrive at the signed trailhead, Granite Point is to your left while straight ahead is Moss Cove, dotted with several small rocky islands. If you are on this trail when the ocean is at low tide, take a look at the offshore rocks, many of which are covered with rockweeds containing so much chlorophyll and other pigments that they appear black. When exposed to the sun at low tide they may look dead and dry but these marine plants have adjusted to life in the intertidal zone and will rehydrate when the high tide returns.

The Moss Cove Trail follows the path of an old road that was used between 1920 and 1926 to haul gravel rocks from the Pit, a small beach located between Coal Chute Point and Granite Point. The gravel was imbedded in what geologists call the Carmelo Formation, a mix of sand, mud and gravel that formed about 60 million years ago when this area was part of a submarine canyon. Around 20 million years ago, tectonic forces moved this portion of the earth's crust upward so that it was alternately exposed to the air, then submerged as the sea level rose and fell. When the sea stayed at one level for a long period, marine terraces and sloping cliffs formed along the ancient shoreline. At Point Lobos, there are two old marine terraces that are still visible. The Moss Cove Trail travels over the lowest and most recent marine terrace, which probably formed about 10,000 years ago.

As the trail follows along the edge of the cove you will travel past the Escobar Rocks. The rocky islands within Moss Cove are named for Don Marcelino Escobar, who in 1839 obtained the land that now includes

Point Lobos as part of an 8,818 acre Mexican Land Grant. A year later, the land was sold for $250, or about 3 cents per acre.

The building to your right is the Hudson House, a ranger residence and docent training center. The house and much of this meadow were once part of the Hudson Ranch, which was added to the reserve in 1976. Historically, this meadow has been grazed by cattle going back perhaps as far as the 1840s. As a result, most of the grasses in the meadow are non-native. To foster a return of native plants and grasses, the park service has used low-intensity, controlled fires to help achieve a diversity of healthy plants and wildlife.

Beginning around the middle of February, the meadow starts to bloom with yellow suncups, creamcups and buttercups, orange-red seaside painted cups, pink-purple checker bloom and pink sea thrift. The California poppy is also common, as is the non-native mustard plant, which grows two to three feet tall and in early summer turns a large portion of the meadow into a sea of yellow.

As you near the end of the trail, your path angles to the left and heads toward Ichxenta Point, which overlooks Monastery Beach and Carmel Bay. Located on the reserve's northern boundary, the point is named after a village occupied by the indigenous people of this area, the Rumsen Ohlone. It is thought their village was located close to San Jose Creek, which enters Carmel Bay at Monastery Beach. Within the reserve, 45 sites have been identified that were used on a seasonal basis by the Ohlone while gathering abalone and mussels or grinding seeds and acorns. One site is

Field mustard

located in the grass between the point and the nearby boundary fence and consists of a relatively flat granite rock with 10 bowl-like mortar cups on its surface. Here, the Ohlone women gathered to grind acorns, which were a staple of their diet. After the acorns were ground and leached of tannic acid, the acorn meal was wrapped in leaves and baked over hot stones or eaten as gruel.

The coastal area immediately north of Ichxenta Point is Carmel River State Beach. Monastery Beach, which takes its name from the Carmelite Monastery on the east side of Highway 1, is located at the south end of the mile-long state beach. There is no access between Point Lobos and the state beach. To return to the trailhead, retrace your steps through the meadow.

Grinding rock near Ichxenta Point.   Photo: Jeff Thomson

Mound Meadow Trail

Trailhead: Next to the paved road across from Hidden Beach.
This trail is also accessible from the entrance road
at the first intersection past the entrance station.

Distance: 0.3 miles

Classification: Easy

*HIGHLIGHTS – This short trail connects Hidden Beach with the
entrance road. It travels along the edge of Mound Meadow, an
ancient marine terrace that formed about 10,000 years ago when the
sea level was higher.*

The Mound Meadow Trail begins across the road from Hidden Beach
and winds along the border of the meadow and a Monterey pine forest.
Although a number of pine trees have spread into the meadow, the
dominant plants are tall non-native annual grasses like wild oats and
little rattlesnake grass, which is distinguished by pouch-like flowers that
resemble rattlesnake tails. Black-tailed deer are common around the
meadow, as are ground squirrels, mice and other small mammals. The
southwestern section of the meadow near Hidden Beach is a nesting
area for killdeer. This bird can be identified by two black chest bands
and by its call, which sounds like its name. You may see this permanent
resident of the reserve feeding in the meadow or along the shoreline
and beaches.

At about the halfway point, your trail crosses the Pine Ridge Trail and
begins a gradual climb into the Monterey pine forest. A short distance
further, you will come to the end of the trail at an intersection with
the Lace Lichen Trail near the entrance road.

North Shore Trail

Trailhead: The Sea Lion Point Parking Area.
This trail is also accessible from its north end
above Whalers Cove.

Distance: 1.4 miles

Classification: Easy

*HIGHLIGHTS — The North Shore Trail leads through an area of
outstanding natural beauty. Along the way, you travel past steep
granite-sided coves, visit one of the last remaining native stands of
Monterey cypress trees at East Grove, and during the spring and
summer, experience close views of nesting sea birds on Guillemot
Island.*

From the Information Station, start off on the Cypress Grove Trail
then, within several steps, turn right onto the North Shore Trail, which
is marked by a sign. Initially, your route passes through an expanse of
coastal scrub plants as it gradually descends to meet the Old Veteran
Trail, a short spur trail to the left that leads to a view of the Old
Veteran, a gnarled and wind-sheared Monterey cypress which clings
to the cliff above Cypress Cove.

Continuing on, the North Shore Trail heads up the low side of Whalers
Knoll under a partial canopy of Monterey pine and Monterey cypress
trees. Veils of lace lichen hang from the lower tree branches, while
along the trail, lizard tail yarrow and seaside daisy plants provide a
splash of color through the summer. After a short climb, you will pass
an intersection with the Whalers Knoll Trail, then descend to an open
area below Big Dome, which forms the north side of Cypress Cove. At
an elevation of 260 feet above sea level, Big Dome is the highest
point in the reserve. It also provides protection from the wind for the
trees that grow in back of it, so unlike the wind-sculpted Monterey
Cypress out on the exposed headlands, the trees in this area grow tall
and symmetrical.

Just ahead, the trail meanders through a level saddle between Big
Dome and Whalers Knoll, where you might see black-tailed deer graz-
ing on shrubs and grass. Then as the trail begins its descent to East
Grove, there is a panoramic view to the northeast across Granite Point,
where on a clear day you can see the Carmelite Monastery's tall spire
rising above the trees in the far distance. From here, your route twists

down the hillside above a small cove, then levels out as it comes to East Grove, the smaller of the two native stands of Monterey cypress found at the reserve. Much like the Monterey cypress trees located on the northeast side of Cypress Cove, the lower branches of many of these trees are covered with an orange-red colored algae called *Trentepohlia.* This is actually a green algae which has a carotene-like pigment that masks its green chlorophyll.

Where the trail comes to a T, a short spur trail leads to the left to an observation area across from Guillemot Island. This small and rocky island is a nesting site for the Brandt's cormorant, pigeon guillemot and western gull. During April and May, Brandt's cormorants establish nests made of seaweed along the ridge and upper flank of the rocky island. The slightly smaller pelagic cormorant prefers to nest in shallow caves along the steep-sided cliffs. Like the cormorants, the pigeon guillemot is a diving bird. It summers at Point Lobos but spends the rest of the year out at sea. This pigeon-sized bird can be recognized by a conspicuous white wing patch on an otherwise black body and by its red feet and red mouth lining. During the spring breeding season, they nest in small cavities on Guillemot Island and in the tunnel below the observation area. Watch closely to see them actually fly, rather than merely swim, underwater.

Bluefish Cove. Photo: Jeff Thomson

Leaving East Grove, the trail enters a Monterey pine forest as it winds along the hillside above Bluefish Cove, which takes its name from a blue-colored rockfish, one of several varieties of rockfish that inhabit this beautiful cove. Divers also report sightings of sunfish, electric rays and an occasional shark. Marine mammals you are likely to see in the cove include sea otters languishing in the kelp forest, and harbor seals.

Before long, you will pass another intersection with the Whalers Knoll Trail, then just ahead, the Whalers Cabin Trail. From there, the North Shore Trail climbs to an overlook high above Whalers Cove, where you have a sweeping view of the reserve's north shore. A few yards further, the path comes to another spur trail which takes off to the left and leads to an overlook of Bluefish Cove. The main trail bears to the right, descends a long stairway and loops around Cannery Point, which in summer is covered by a carpet of yellow-flowered lizard tail yarrow and lavender seaside daisy. The point is named for an abalone cannery which operated from 1900 to 1928, located at what is now the Whalers Cove Parking Area.

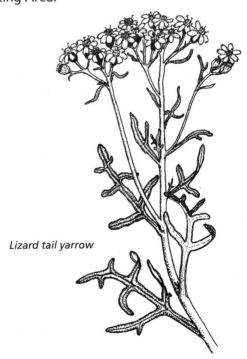

Lizard tail yarrow

Pine Ridge Trail

Trailhead: Piney Woods Picnic Area

Distance: 0.7 miles

Classification: Easy

HIGHLIGHTS – From the Piney Woods Picnic Area, this trail travels through a forest of Monterey pine trees to its end at the South Plateau Trail. Along the way, there are good views of Mound Meadow and the reserve's southern coastline.

From the picnic area, a short spur trail climbs the hillside to the main trail. A left turn at this intersection leads to the Lace Lichen Trail, which heads over to the entrance road. The main portion of the trail goes to the right and meanders along the edge of a Monterey pine forest. Before long, your path comes to a bench with an open view of Mound Meadow and Weston Beach in the distance.

Continuing on, the trail winds along the contour of a ridge as it passes through the Monterey pine forest, one of only three natural stands of this tree in California. Monterey pines grow rapidly and can be recognized by shiny green needles that develop in groups of three. Their cones are an important source of food for the western gray squirrel, which might be seen scampering in the branches overhead. Common plants through this section of the trail include coffeeberry, bracken fern, sticky monkey flower, hedge nettle, and hairy honeysuckle.

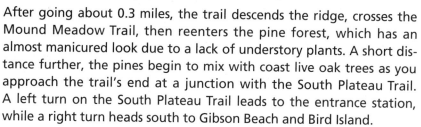

Coffeeberry

After going about 0.3 miles, the trail descends the ridge, crosses the Mound Meadow Trail, then reenters the pine forest, which has an almost manicured look due to a lack of understory plants. A short distance further, the pines begin to mix with coast live oak trees as you approach the trail's end at a junction with the South Plateau Trail. A left turn on the South Plateau Trail leads to the entrance station, while a right turn heads south to Gibson Beach and Bird Island.

Sand Hill Trail

Trailhead: 0.1 miles west of the Sea Lion Point Parking Area on the Sea Lion Point Trail.

Distance: 0.2 miles

Classification: Easy. The section of this trail which connects with the paved road is wheelchair accessible.

HIGHLIGHTS – The Sand Hill Trail travels along the ocean bluff between Sea Lion Cove and Sand Hill Cove. It offers excellent vantage points for viewing marine mammals plus great views of the coastline.

The Sand Hill Trail begins at an intersection with the Sea Lion Point Trail about 0.1 miles west of the Sea Lion Point Parking Area. From the bluff above Sea Lion Cove, the trail climbs briefly, then quickly levels out for an easy walk. Along the way you can look down on Sea Lion Cove for a birds-eye view of harbor seals hauled out on the rocks or sea otters floating in the kelp beds. If you have binoculars, look out to the large white-capped rocks in the distance where, most of the year, you can spot groups of sea lions.

Sea Lion Cove. Photo: Jeff Thomson

Just ahead, the trail will pass a 60-million-year-old boulder consisting of thousands of round stones held together in a "cement" of sandstone. By walking around the lower side of the boulder you can see how it has eroded into something resembling a prehistoric bus stop bench. Looking south down the coast, there is a splendid view of the Carmel Highlands area with Soberanes Point in the distance.

For much of its length, the Sand Hill Trail is bordered by plants associated with the coastal bluff community. Plants in this zone have adapted to survive in an environment of almost continuous winds, salt spray, periods of heavy rain and times of drought. Most of these plants have developed a low, mat-like appearance and because they grow in shallow and porous soil many of them have developed small leathery or waxy leaves to reduce evaporation. Some of the coastal bluff plants you will see along the trail include buckwheat, sagewort, rattle-weed, with its distinctive seed pods, and seaside painted cup.

Soon after the trail bends to the left and heads inland, you have a good view of Sand Hill Cove, which is another place to spot harbor seals. Bird watchers might see pelagic cormorants nesting in small cavities on the face of the bluff, as well as cliff swallows or violet-green swallows darting about.

Continuing on, your path passes a connection with the South Shore Trail, which drops off to the right. Past this intersection, the Sand Hill Trail travels through a coastal scrub plant community dominated by woody-stemmed plants like coyote bush, poison oak and California sage. In short order, the trail comes to its end at the paved road just below the Sea Lion Point Parking Area.

Sea Lion Point Trail

Trailhead: Sea Lion Point Parking Area

Distance: 0.6 miles round trip

Classification: Easy. An "easy access" trail is being planned to make much of this trail wheelchair accessible.

HIGHLIGHTS – This trail spotlights one of the main attractions of the reserve, the California sea lion. In addition, you will probably see harbor seals and maybe a sea otter or two. The Sea Lion Point Trail also offers a look into this area's geologic past.

The well-trod path to Sea Lion Point begins on the west side of the parking area and is marked by a trail sign. You will start off under a canopy of young Monterey cypress trees, then quickly emerge into the open and walk through a coastal scrub plant community. This section of the trail is lined with a dense growth of coyote bush, aromatic California sagebrush, silvery sagewort, buckwheat, hedge nettle and the almost ever-present poison oak. A couple of other flowering plants you may see are sticky monkey flower which sends forth a profusion of orange blossoms starting in late spring, and seaside painted cup, one of two species of paintbrush found at the reserve. You will see its bright red flowers if you visit the reserve between March and May.

The most conspicuous bird along this trail is the white-crowned sparrow, whose preferred habitat is the bushy scrub. It feeds on seeds and insects along the path and can be recognized by bold black and white stripes on its head. When the coastal scrub plants are blooming in spring and summer, look for iridescent hummingbirds streaking by or hovering over a flower. Yellow-rumped warblers are also common along this path.

Down to your right is Headland Cove, a good place to spot harbor seals, which often haul themselves up on the beach at low tide. Like the sea lion, harbor seals have developed a layer of fat to keep warm in the chilly ocean water.

Harbor seal. Photo: Chuck Bancroft

However, they differ from the sea lion in that they are smaller in size, have a less flexible spine and a shorter neck, and are much less vocal.

The southern sea otter may also be seen floating in the canopy of the kelp forest within Headland Cove. Unlike the sea lion and harbor seal, this marine mammal has not developed a layer of insulating fat.

A resting sea otter.

Photo:
Richard Bucich

Instead, the sea otter has dense fur which traps air next to the skin to keep it dry and warm. About the only parts of their body not covered by fur are their foot pads, which is why a resting sea otter will usually be seen with its forepaws and hindflippers poking up out of the water into the warmer air. Another way they stay warm is by maintaining a high metabolism. An adult otter will eat about 25% of its body weight each day.

As you walk along the trail, expect to be greeted by a California ground squirrel standing up on its hind legs and begging for a snack. They are cute and sociable animals, so it may be hard to resist the temptation to feed them but please do not. They do well on their natural diet of seeds and plants, and might bite if you offer them a snack. The ground squirrel is probably the most noticeable small mammal at the reserve and attracts predators such as hawks, bobcats and coyotes. Sentinel squirrels will station themselves at a lookout point, and, when frightened, make a chirping bark of alarm until the danger passes.

In short order, the trail reaches a rocky crest which overlooks Sea Lion Point, Devil's Cauldron and Sea Lion Rocks. After descending the stairs to the point, turn around and look at the weathered rock outcroppings on the hillside. This remarkable landscape is an ancient deposit of sand and gravel which settled on the underlying granodiorite about 60 million years ago when this area was part of a deep submarine canyon. Over time, it hardened into a sandstone that geologists call the Carmelo Formation.

At the bottom of the stairway, the trail heads straight to an opening in the guide wire railing, then begins a counter-clockwise loop around Sea Lion Point, or as it was called by early Spanish explorers, Punta De Los Lobos Marinos, Point of the Sea Wolves. For many people the supreme effect of a visit to the reserve is experienced on this rocky point jutting out into the Pacific Ocean. To your left and right the ocean surges against the point, while straight ahead the waters churn and froth in the Devil's Cauldron. Most of the year, California sea lions can be heard barking from their perch on a group of rocky islands in the distance appropriately named Sea Lion Rocks. From August to June, hundreds of mostly male sea lions live at Point Lobos. In early summer, the sexually mature males head south to breed with females in the Channel Islands.

Sea lions.   Photo: Chuck Bancroft

Continuing around the point, you will have another good view of the steep cliffs above Sea Lion Cove. Since it faces south and is protected by Sea Lion Point, the water in the cove is relatively calm. Harbor seals can frequently be seen sunning themselves on the flat rock in the middle of the cove or lying on the beach. Near the end of the trail where it returns to the low area at the base of the cliffs, take a look to your left. Beyond the eroded rock formations, waves pound against the shore in marked contrast to the calm waters of Sea Lion Cove. At low tide, you might find purple and green sea urchins, pink coraline algae, limpets, and goose barnacles in the tide pools, plus shore crabs dancing sideways along the rocks. If you decide to explore the tidepools, be extremely careful and keep a close eye on the waves. Never turn your back on the ocean, since unpredictable large waves can suddenly appear and wash you off the rocks. Also, please remember this is a state reserve, so collecting, disturbing or removing any natural object is not allowed.

After climbing back up the hillside, return the way you came or turn right and loop back to the parking area by taking the Sand Hill Trail, which heads south along the cliff then turns inland and ends at the paved road just below the parking lot.

South Plateau Trail

Trailhead: The entrance station

Distance: 0.7 miles

Classification: Easy

HIGHLIGHTS – Starting from the entrance station, this trail winds through a shady forest on its way to the beautiful white sands of Gibson Beach and China Cove. A special guide to plant life along the trail is available at the trailhead.

The South Plateau Trail begins on the left side of the road just past the entrance station, and immediately enters the shade of a Monterey pine and coast live oak forest. The path is littered with pine needles and bordered by a healthy under-story of poison oak and wild blackberry, which resembles poison oak except for its sharp spines. Another common plant along the trail is hedge nettle or wood mint. It has fuzzy leaves and lavender flowers which blossom between February and June.

Wild blackberry

After going a short distance, you begin an easy climb up and along the side of Rat Hill, which is named for the abundance of dusky-footed wood rat nests on its slope. Descending along the hillside, the trail winds through an area which supports a fairly large number of Douglas iris, whose purple-blue flowers herald the coming of spring. During the summer months, this section of the trail is also accented with the orange blossoms of sticky monkey flower.

Soon after passing an intersection with the Pine Ridge Trail, your path climbs up and over a low ridge then down to a grassy swale which contains a number of large Monterey pines. From here, the trail begins to climb Vierra's Knoll, named after the Vierra family who once had a home and farm in this vicinity. John Vierra was one of the Portuguese whalers who arrived at Point Lobos in the early 1860s.

After the whaling industry declined in the 1880s, many of the whalers stayed and established small farms. Since the family farm had a surplus of milk, Mr. Vierra's mother-in-law wrote home to the Azores for a cheese recipe. Sometime shortly after 1900, the recipe found its way to the David Jacks Dairy just north of Monterey. They shipped the cheese to San Francisco, where it soon became popular and known as Monterey Jack Cheese.

After cresting Vierra's Knoll, the trail emerges from the forest and twists down to a breathtaking view of the ocean and rocky headlands south of the reserve. Just ahead, you will come to a spur trail on the left which leads to a staircase that descends to Gibson Beach. The beautiful white sands of Gibson Beach are the result of decomposing granodiorite rocks that surround the cove. During much of the year, it is possible to spot sea otters floating in the canopy of the offshore kelp forest. Following winter storms, tangled masses of kelp often wash up on the beach. The decomposing kelp attracts swarms of insects which provide food for shorebirds like the black turnstone. These birds nest on the Alaskan coastal tundra in summer and visit the Pacific shore in fall and winter. They can be recognized by their short legs, black plumage and white belly. At the far end of the beach is Gibson Creek, which forms the reserve's southern boundary.

The South Plateau Trail ends a few yards past the spur trail to Gibson Beach, where it meets the Bird Island Trail, which comes in from your right. If you continue straight ahead, the Bird Island Trail quickly reaches Pelican Point and an overlook of Bird Island. A right turn on the Bird Island Trail leads to a staircase above the emerald-green waters of China Cove. From there, it travels north along the headland to a picnic area and parking lot at the Bird Island Trailhead.

South Shore Trail

Trailhead: This trail can be accessed at its north end near the Sea Lion Point Parking Area, at its south end at the Bird Island Parking Area, and from a number of pull-outs along the road.

Distance: 1 mile

Classification: Easy

HIGHLIGHTS – Travel along the ocean's edge past an ever-changing pattern of low cliffs and wave-sculpted coves.

Unlike the granite headlands of the reserve's northern shoreline, most of the south shore is comprised of a softer mix of sandstone and gravel. Over the past several thousand years, ocean waves have worn away the sandstone to create a string of beautiful coves, crevices and shelves.

Probably the most photogenic cove along the trail is the one at Weston Beach, which has been recorded in stunning photos by Ansel Adams and Edward Weston, for whom this beach is named. Much of what attracted these men and countless other artists is revealed only at low tide when the ocean recedes to expose varicolored sandstone which has eroded into a fascinating pattern of miniature ridges and troughs. Another

The South Shore Trail above Headland Cove.   Photo: Jeff Thomson

interesting feature of Weston Beach is how horizontal layers of sedimentary rock at the north side of the cove change position and become nearly vertical at the south end. This phenomenon is probably the result of the rock folding and breaking about 20 million years ago as it moved northward along what we now call the San Andreas fault system.

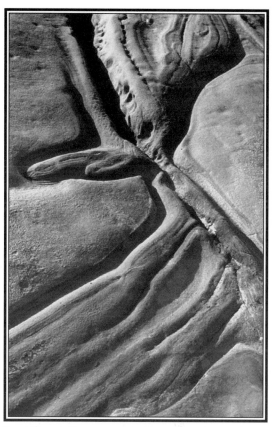

Sandstone patterns. Photo: Jeff Thomson

At several locations along the South Shore Trail, you can view fascinating intertidal creatures in pools that form when the ocean recedes at low tide. The most common inhabitants of these tide pools are invertebrates: small snails, periwinkles, barnacles and shore crabs. You may also see red and purple sea urchins and flower-like anemones. Upon close inspection, you might even spot a sculpin, one of the few fish species that inhabit the intertidal zone on a year-round basis. Sculpins are about 3 inches in length and camouflaged to match their environment. They blend so well with their surroundings that it is a challenge to distinguish them from the rocks and fronds of red, brown and green algae. If you venture out on the rocks to observe the tidepools, walk carefully for your own safety and to spare the marine life underfoot. Also, keep a close eye on the waves and remember to never turn your back on the ocean. Since this is a state reserve, disturbing, collecting and removing any natural object is not allowed.

Purple sea urchin. Photo: Jerry Loomis

As you walk along the trail, chances are good that you will see shore-birds feeding along the surfline. Some of them are year-round residents at the reserve while others visit on a seasonal basis or merely stop here briefly on their migration to more distant locations. A few of the more commonly-seen shorebirds are American black oystercatchers, willets and killdeer. Summer visitors to the reserve may also see ocean birds flying low across the water on their way to feeding grounds or nesting sites.

Plant life on the South Shore Trail consists of woody-stemmed coastal scrub and bluff plants which stabilize the soil and provide home and shelter for a variety of small animals. During the late spring and summer months, many of these plants are in bloom and provide a colorful backdrop of lavender, yellow, orange and white.

Whalers Cabin Trail

Trailhead: Next to the Whalers Cabin Museum
Distance: 0.1 miles
Classification: Moderate

HIGHLIGHTS – This short trail provides a connection from the Whalers Cabin to the North Shore Trail and Bluefish Cove.

From the signed trailhead located just few yards north of Whalers Cabin, you will first climb through coastal scrub vegetation, then quickly enter the cover of a Monterey pine forest. A short distance further, the trail ends at an intersection with the North Shore Trail.

A left turn on the North Shore Trail leads to the parking area near Sea Lion Point and the Information Station. Along the way, you travel through East Grove, one of two native stands of Monterey Cypress trees at Point Lobos. If you have a limited amount of time, turn right on the North Shore Trail. After going a short distance, the trail climbs to an overlook of Whalers Cove, then descends to Cannery Point, which offers an excellent view of Granite Point and Whalers Cove. To complete your loop, walk down the stairs to Whalers Cove Parking Area and follow the paved road back to Whalers Cabin.

Whalers Knoll Trail

Trailhead: Three short trails climb Whalers Knoll.
One starts on the entrance road and two
begin on the North Shore Trail.

Distance: 0.2 miles one way. 0.5 miles to traverse the knoll.

Classification: Moderate

*HIGHLIGHTS – From the bench atop **Whalers Knoll** you will find excellent views of tree-covered headlands framed by the blue Pacific.*

The trails to Whalers Knoll are relatively short (about 0.2 miles one way) and climb through a forest of Monterey pine trees. Along the way, you might see a western gray squirrel pursuing a meal of pine nuts or glimpse a black-tailed deer browsing in the understory. During the winter months, look for monarch butterflies that congregate on tree branches which are exposed to the sun and sheltered from the wind.

If you are walking up to the viewpoint on the trail that starts from the entrance road, stay to the left at each trail intersection; otherwise, you will miss the summit and end up at Bluefish Cove. On the trail that begins at Bluefish Cove, stay to the right at each split in the trail. From the Sea Lion Point Parking Area, take the North Shore Trail, then turn right on the Whalers Knoll Trail, which twists up the hillside a short distance to the overlook.

Upon reaching the summit overlook, which is marked by a wood bench, you are treated to a spectacular view. Straight ahead, Big Dome spills down to the Pacific, while to the right, on a clear day you can see the Carmel coastline and green fairways of the Pebble Beach Golf Course. To the left, your view is southwest toward Sea Lion Cove and Sand Hill Cove. On most days, you can also hear the sound of barking sea lions wafting up from their offshore perch on Sea Lion Rocks.

Back in the 1860s and 70s, when a shore whaling station was operating out of what is now Whalers Cove, a flagpole was positioned on this 240-foot-high knoll. When a passing whale was spotted, a lookout raised a signal flag to alert the boat crew down at the cove. Once out on the open waves, the crew watched for the flag to be dipped as a signal they were going in the right direction. To learn more about the history of whaling activities at Point Lobos, visit the Whaling Station Museum located at Whalers Cove. There you will find displays of whaling equipment and exhibit panels describing the lives of the whalers and their families.

How You Can Help the Reserve...

Join the Point Lobos Natural History Association

The Point Lobos Natural History Association is a nonprofit organization formed to enhance the public's awareness of the unique qualities of Point Lobos. Membership fees are reinvested in public education and service activities, such as developing and supporting docent training, publishing and distributing interpretive materials, conducting school and public nature walk programs, and maintaining interpretive centers like the Information Station, the Whalers Cabin and the Whaling Station Museums.

Your Membership Benefits include:
• Quarterly PLNHA Newsletter
• 20% discount on all items sold by the association
• Voting privileges in the association
• Participation in association meetings and special programs

Please join. Fill out the application below and return it with your check. New memberships are valid for one year from sign-up.

Send to: Point Lobos Natural History Association, Route 1 Box 62, Carmel, CA 93923.

Point Lobos Natural History Association
MEMBERSHIP APPLICATION

NAME

ADDRESS

CITY   STATE   ZIP

PHONE   FAX

Annual Membership Dues:

❏ Student $ 5   ❏ Patron $100
❏ Individual $10   ❏ Contributing $250
❏ Family $15   ❏ Donor $500
❏ Sustaining $30   ❏ Life $1,000
❏ Supporting $50

NOTES

Order Form

Please send me _____ copies of **Explore...***Point Lobos State Reserve* @ $10.95 per copy.

DATE
_____

NAME
_____

MAILING ADDRESS
_____

CITY _____ STATE _____ ZIP _____

DAYTIME TELEPHONE
_____

Quantity: _____ (x $10.95) = $ _____

CA residents add sales tax of 88¢ per book $ _____

Shipping $ _____

TOTAL $ _____

Shipping:
$2.50 for the first book and 75¢
for each additional book.

Send Check or Money Order to:
Walkabout Publications
P. O. Box 1299, Soquel, CA 95073
(408) 462-3370
(As of April 1998, phone prefix will change to 831)

Satisfaction Guaranteed or
Your Money Back!

Walkabout
Publications

Also Available from Walkabout Publications

Explore...The Forest of Nisene Marks State Park. A visitor's guide to one of the most historically interesting and geologically significant redwood parks in central California.

Please send me _____ copies of *Explore...The Forest of Nisene Marks State Park* @ $9.95 per copy.

DATE _____

NAME _____

MAILING ADDRESS _____

CITY _____ STATE _____ ZIP _____

DAYTIME TELEPHONE _____

Quantity: _____ (x $9.95) = $ _____

CA residents add sales tax of 80¢ per book $ _____

Shipping $ _____

TOTAL $ _____

Shipping:
$2.50 for the first book and 75¢
for each additional book.

Send Check or Money Order to:
Walkabout Publications
P.O. Box 1299, Soquel, CA 95073
(408) 462-3370
(As of April 1998, phone prefix will change to 831)

*Satisfaction Guaranteed or
Your Money Back!*

 **W**alkabout Publications